DISCOVER*LIFE*

Nehemiah
A Servant Leader

LEADER'S GUIDE
by
Alvin J. Vander Griend
revised by
Drew Gordon

FAITH ALIVE
Christian Resources
Grand Rapids, Michigan

Unless otherwise indicated, the Scripture quotations in this publication are from the HOLY BIBLE, NEW INTERNATIONAL VERSION, © 1973, 1978, 1984, International Bible Society. Used by permission of Zondervan Bible Publishers.

Cover photo by Stone.

Faith Alive Christian Resources published by CRC Publications.

We welcome your comments. Call us at 1-800-333-8300 or e-mail us at editors@faithaliveresources.org.

ISBN 1-56212-574-5

10 9 8 7 6 5 4 3 2 1

Contents

How to Use This Guide

Discover Life is a small group outreach Bible study ministry. It gives spiritually mature members of the church a way to reach out to friends, relatives, neighbors, work associates, and others who need to come to Christ, grow spiritually in Christ, and enjoy the fellowship of the body of Christ.

Following are ten strategy guidelines to keep in mind when organizing Discover Life groups.

1. **Meet at times that fit people's schedules.** Don't expect all the people you want to reach to come together at the same time or on the same day. Personal schedules will vary a great deal. A church that wants to reach many people should have groups meeting in the morning, in the evening, on Saturday, at lunchtime, and even on Sunday.
2. **Lead the groups with a team of at least two.** Make sure you have leadership depth and strength. Group leaders are busy people and do not have much available time. Work and family activities usually take precedence over Bible study. Leadership will be stronger and the group more likely to succeed with a leadership team. Leaders working together can share the load of leadership, give each other mutual support, cover for each other, and recruit from their acquaintances.
3. **Meet at convenient, nonthreatening places.** People who don't go to church will feel more comfortable in a familiar environment such as a restaurant, boardroom, or conference room than in a church. Try to meet in "neutral territory" where people will feel comfortable.
4. **Invite prospective members for a definite short-term period.** Many people are wary of long-term commitments. After the first series of lessons is complete, take a break and then invite them again for another series. Keep repeating this as long as members are interested. Discover Life material is designed for short-term studies.
5. **Require no advance homework or prior knowledge of the Bible.** Requiring homework will build a cycle of defeat into participants. Busy people who are not able to prepare will stay home rather than risk embarrassment. To avoid this, do not make advance assignments. Make it clear that the group will start fresh with the material at the beginning of each meeting.

   Tear the lesson pages out of the study guides and hand them out as single sheets at the beginning of the meeting. Begin with the approach question (the first question) to warm members up to the subject. Read the first Bible passage and then allow a brief silent study time so members can get oriented to the material and prepare to answer the first inductive questions. AfterWord provides optional material after the lesson.

   Be careful not to assume members' prior knowledge of the Bible. Those without a church background will soon feel left out of any discussion that draws on prior knowledge. Stick with the passage at hand and relate it to life. In this way everybody is on the same level.
6. **Recruit by personally inviting friends and acquaintances.** Very few people come to a group through newspaper ads, posters, or flyer announcements. The most successful invitation is a personal one from a friend or acquaintance who offers to take that person to the group meeting.
7. **Put a lot of effort into building relationships.** The concern of those who come will not be "How much can I learn here?" but "How well am I accepted as a member of this group?" They will not so much ask "Is this true?" as "How does this group make me feel?" Respond to their concern by reaching out to them and becoming a channel of Christ's love to them. Invest time and energy before, after, and between meetings; get to know those who come. Good meetings are not enough; you need growing relationships too.
8. **Use appropriate materials.** Most people are used to dealing with letter-size black-on-white pages. Discover Life material is designed with this in mind. Including the Bible passage as part of the lesson gives nonchurched people, who may not want to be seen carrying a Bible, the option of carrying a pad holder in which they can keep the single-sheet lessons. Including the Bible passage also avoids embarrassing those who do not know their way around the Bible, and it gives everyone a common version to work from.
9. **Help group members discover truths from the Bible for themselves.** People don't like to be told what to think. They prefer to make up their minds after examining the evidence. They are also more likely to believe what they discover for themselves. The inductive questions in the Discover Life lessons make it possible for group members to discover for themselves what the Bible says. The leader's material encourages the leader to keep asking questions as the group moves more deeply into the passage and applies the truth to their lives.
10. **Make sure that Bible truths are related to life.** When studying the Bible, people are usually concerned about knowing what it means for their life. They tend to lose interest in an abstract discussion. To help keep the discussions life-oriented, we have included a number of application questions in the leader's guide.

Optional Study Elements

Depending on the goals and makeup of your group, the Optional Prayer Time and Optional Accountability Question may be incorporated into your Bible study. These two elements are designed to establish a more relational dynamic in your group.

Optional Prayer Time. In the leader's guide, each session includes a suggested format for group sharing and prayer. Be sure you create an environment where individuals don't feel forced to share prayer requests or to pray aloud. Never ask someone to pray without checking with them ahead of time. You may experiment to find an approach that works best for you. In some cases you may ask individuals to pair off to pray. If you meet in a public place such as a restaurant, you may want to distribute index cards on which group members can write their prayer items and then have members swap cards for individual prayer throughout the week.

Optional Accountability Question. For spiritual growth to occur, it is essential that group members apply lessons learned to their own lives. That is the purpose of the Optional Accountability Question. Don't feel that you must use the suggested question if one of your own better fits your group. However, accountability suggests follow-up. There are several ways you might follow up on the Accountability Question. One is to have individuals write their accountability issue for the week on an index card and hand it to the leader. The next time you meet, these cards are distributed to the group members, who pair off for a few minutes to discuss how things went. Another approach is for each group member to hand the card to another individual. The next week those two will pair up to share for a few minutes.

And Finally

Whether you are leading a group in your workplace, in your home, or in another setting, the following guidelines should assist you in your leadership role.

1. **Pray.** Nothing will prepare you for leadership more than prayer. Pray for God's direction in making organizational decisions. Pray for the Holy Spirit's direction in whom to invite and for a positive response from those invited. Pray faithfully for group members, and pray for your eyes to be opened to the truths in God's Word and how those truths can best be communicated to your small group. Remember: "More things are wrought by prayer than this world ever dreamed of."

2. **Prepare.** First, **prepare yourself.** The leader's guide for each discussion is thorough and reinforces the discovery method of Bible study. We suggest highlighting key phrases or questions for easy reference as you prepare. Take your leader's guide with you to the group and be relaxed and informal about using it while you are leading. The perforated discussion copies, located in the study guides, are to be removed and given to group members each week. If you freely show you have extra help in preparing for the discussion, your group members may dare to ask their questions more readily. They'll see it's not that you're smart and they're ignorant, or that the discussion is just an unguided free-for-all, but that it is planned and focused. Be sure you focus on the discussion element, rather than become a teacher with the "answer book."

   Second, **prepare your group.** State the ground rules before you begin the group. You may need to repeat them as new members join. This will help group members know how the discussion will proceed and what will be expected of them. Here are some basic guidelines:

   - We're here to see what the Bible has to say, not to argue opinions.
   - No previous experience in studying the Bible is needed.
   - This discussion will not require homework or outside preparation.
   - Respect the confidentiality of the group and affirm each group member. "What we say here must stay here."

3. **Persevere.** It takes time to build relationships. The Holy Spirit may already be at work in some of your group members, and they will respond eagerly. Others will be wary. Still others may be in such pain, they'll come because they are desperate. Accept the people God gives you—unconditionally. Often God's timetable is not the same as ours, but be confident that God will use your efforts. Modeling Christ's love may be the most important thing you do. Relax and watch the Spirit work!

Introduction

The fate of the free world hangs each day on the attentiveness and skill of the United States Secret Service. They protect the president and other high government officials from people who are always watching for weaknesses they can exploit to cause harm and wreak havoc.

How many Secret Service officers do you know by name? It's probably the same number as that of the royal cupbearers and food tasters you can remember from history. The fact is, most people don't go down in history for doing their job well. Yet the foundation of the next generation is laid with our hard work and skillful service today.

Nehemiah was the royal cupbearer to the king of Persia, the chief world power of that time. The cupbearer was a servant, and yet his integrity was critical. His job was to detect any poison in his master's drink before it was served. Yet Nehemiah was a servant leader whose strength of character went far beyond the norm, and who eventually made a difference in world history.

Like Nehemiah, we all have important jobs to do, and as long as we do a pretty good job most of us go relatively unnoticed. But, also like Nehemiah, God has put us in a strategic position according to a larger plan. What will keep us ready for the watershed decisions of our lives, for the pivotal events? How will we stay focused as we face frequent discouragement and opposition? What will keep us going when we lose sight of the big picture and are consumed with the daily grind?

These seven studies give clear principles for cupbearers—for us average people who nonetheless want to make a difference in our families and communities. We want to set an example that might nourish the next generation when times are tough. We want to be genuinely successful in a way that won't be erased by the sands of time.

May God bless your step of faith as you study these biblical principles; may God make them come alive for you.

DISCOVER*LIFE*

Success for the Asking

Lesson 1

1. **If you could ask for one major change in your country or community or family, what would you ask for?**

   What difference would it make knowing that the person you asked had complete power to grant your request?

   How much effort would you be willing to invest if you knew that your request could not fail?

Transitional Comment

Nehemiah had a very difficult task to do. But since God had laid this task on his heart and had promised to be with him, Nehemiah was confident of success.

2. **Nehemiah 1:1-4**

1The words of Nehemiah son of Hacaliah:

In the month of Kislev in the twentieth year, while I was in the citadel of Susa, 2Hanani, one of my brothers, came from Judah with some other men, and I questioned them about the Jewish remnant that survived the exile, and also about Jerusalem.

3They said to me, "Those who survived the exile and are back in the province are in great trouble and disgrace. The wall of Jerusalem is broken down, and its gates have been burned with fire."

4When I heard these things, I sat down and wept. For some days I mourned and fasted and prayed before the God of heaven.

Introductory Comment

Nehemiah, an exiled Jew who served as cupbearer of the Persian king Artaxerxes, was moved to tears when he heard of the trouble and shame of his people in Jerusalem.

Questions

a. **What does Hanani report concerning Jerusalem?**

   Why was a city wall important in those days?

b. **How does Nehemiah react to the news, and what does that tell us about him?**

   Where does he take his concern first of all?

   How do people usually first respond when problems arise?

Helpful Notes

- *Jerusalem.* The capital and worship center of ancient Israel. This city was the focus of Israel's hopes for restoring the nation.
- *Kislev.* November-December.
- *twentieth year.* Twentieth year of the reign of King Artaxerxes, about 445 years before Christ.
- *Susa.* Capital of the Medo-Persian empire.
- *prayed.* To understand Nehemiah as a man of prayer, see Nehemiah 2:4; 4:4-5; 5:19; and 6:9.
- *remnant.* Refers to the small number of Israelites remaining in Palestine.
- *wall of Jerusalem is broken down.* The Jews had tried to rebuild the wall earlier in Artaxerxes's reign, but the king had ordered them to stop (Ezra 4:7-23). Without a wall they were defenseless against their enemies.

3. **Nehemiah 1:5-11**

5Then I said:

"O LORD, God of heaven, the great and awesome God, who keeps his covenant of love with those who love him and obey his commands, 6let your ear be attentive and your eyes open to hear the prayer your servant is praying before you day and night for your servants, the people of Israel. I confess the sins we Israelites, including myself and my father's house, have committed against you. 7We have acted very wickedly toward you. We have not obeyed the commands, decrees and laws you gave your servant Moses.

8"Remember the instruction you gave your servant Moses, saying, 'If you are unfaithful, I will scatter you among the nations, 9but if you return to me and obey my commands, then even if your exiled people are at the farthest horizon, I will gather them from there and bring them to the place I have chosen as a dwelling for my Name.'

10"They are your servants and your people, whom you redeemed by your great strength and your mighty hand. 11O Lord, let your ear be attentive to the prayer of this your servant and to the prayer of your servants who delight in revering your name. Give your servant success today by granting him favor in the presence of this man."

I was cupbearer to the king.

Introductory Comment

Mourning and fasting, Nehemiah went to God with the problem on his heart.

Questions

a. **How does Nehemiah address God?**

   What do the opening phrases of Nehemiah's prayer tell us about God? About Nehemiah's attitude toward God?

   What might be a contemporary example of a "covenant of love"? With whom does God keep his covenant?

   How would you address God if you spoke to him?

b. **What does Nehemiah confess?**

   Whose sin does he confess?

Why does he make this confession?

Why might admitting personal fault be important in solving a problem?

c. What promise does Nehemiah claim, and why?

How is this promise related to his situation?

How was the scattering of the people evidence that God keeps all his promises? Why does Nehemiah take heart in this?

d. What does he ask for himself?

Was Nehemiah right in asking God for success? Why?

Have you ever prayed, "Lord, make me successful"? When would it be right to pray this? When would it be wrong?

e. What does a cupbearer or food taster for royalty actually do?

How important is the job?

What kind of person would be chosen for such a job?

Helpful Notes

- *covenant of love.* Nehemiah appeals to God's nature, since God is the only one who can both make a promise to people and guarantee the power necessary to keep that promise over many generations. Nehemiah acknowledges that God is powerful, has integrity in keeping his promises, and is loving and faithful toward his people.
- *decrees.* Public proclamation expressing God's will.
- *instruction you gave Moses.* See Deuteronomy 29:25-30:5.
- *place I have chosen.* Jerusalem, where God's temple was first located and later rebuilt.
- *redeemed.* Freed from the slavery of Egypt.
- *this man.* Artaxerxes, king of Persia.
- *cupbearer.* One who chose and tasted the king's wine to make certain it was not poisoned. The cupbearer was usually a person of influence in the court.

4. Nehemiah 2:1-6

1In the month of Nisan in the twentieth year of King Artaxerxes, when wine was brought for him, I took the wine and gave it to the king. I had not been sad in his presence before; 2so the king asked me, "Why does your face look so sad when you are not ill? This can be nothing but sadness of heart."

I was very much afraid, 3but I said to the king, "May the king live forever! Why should my face not look sad when the city where my fathers are buried lies in ruins, and its gates have been destroyed by fire?"

4The king said to me, "What is it you want?"

Then I prayed to the God of heaven, 5and I answered the king, "If it pleases the king and if your servant has found favor in his sight, let him send me to the city in Judah where my fathers are buried so that I can rebuild it."

6Then the king, with the queen sitting beside him, asked me, "How long will your journey take, and when will you get back?" It pleased the king to send me; so I set a time.

Introductory Comment

Four months after Nehemiah first heard the news from Jerusalem, he spoke to King Artaxerxes about the problem.

Questions

a. Would you consider Nehemiah fearful or bold? Why?

Can you remember a time when you needed to make an important request of someone in authority? What went through your mind?

What about Nehemiah's usual demeanor prompted the king to ask him what was wrong?

b. How does God give Nehemiah the success he had prayed for?

What connection do we see here between prayer and action?

How should prayer and action be combined in our lives?

c. What insight do we gain into Nehemiah's prayer life from verse 4?

How does Nehemiah's prayer in 2:4 differ from his prayer in 1:5-11?

What does this tell us about the diverse nature of prayer? How might it change people's stereotype of prayer?

What are the greatest hindrances to prayer?

Helpful Notes

- *Nisan.* March-April. Nehemiah waited and prayed for four months before speaking to the king.
- *I had not been sad in his presence before.* The king's servants were supposed to display a cheerful disposition.
- *fathers are buried.* Jerusalem was the ancestral burial place for Nehemiah's family.
- *the king . . . asked me.* No one spoke in the Persian court unless spoken to by the king.

5. Nehemiah 2:7-10

7I also said to him, "If it pleases the king, may I have letters to the governors of Trans-Euphrates, so that they will provide me safe-conduct until I arrive in Judah? 8And may I have a letter to Asaph, keeper of the king's forest, so he will give me timber to make beams for the gates of the citadel by the temple and for the city wall and for the residence I will occupy?" And because the gracious hand of my God was upon me, the king granted my requests. 9So I went to the governors of Trans-Euphrates and gave them the king's letters. The king had also sent army officers and cavalry with me.

10When Sanballat the Horonite and Tobiah the Ammonite official heard about this, they were very much disturbed that someone had come to promote the welfare of the Israelites.

Introductory Comment

Having received the king's approval, Nehemiah requests the king's help in some very important ways.

Questions

a. **How does Nehemiah show forethought and careful planning?**

b. **How does Nehemiah account for the king's consent to his request?**

How can we be sure of God's approval of our plans and activities?

c. **What hostile reaction does Nehemiah encounter?**

Why do you suppose these two regional governors were disturbed?

Is it normal to experience opposition in bold ventures like this? Explain.

Should those who move God's plan forward expect opposition? Why?

Helpful Notes

- *letters.* Orders to government officials who would be able to help Nehemiah on his journey.
- *Trans-Euphrates.* The area beyond the Euphrates River, encompassing all of Palestine and Syria.
- *king's forests.* Probably oak, poplar, and terebinth forests a few miles south of Jerusalem.
- *Sanballat.* Governor of Samaria (not far from Jerusalem) and chief political opponent of Nehemiah.
- *Tobiah.* Probably the governor of the territory across the Jordan River from Judah and Jerusalem.

Main Ideas

- Talking to God and relying on God's promises was an integral part of Nehemiah's everyday life.
- Nehemiah combined prayer with godly action in pursuing a God-inspired goal.
- In time, God gave Nehemiah success by moving King Artaxerxes to respond in a very favorable way.
- Being a servant leader does not mean powerlessness; in fact, faithful service plus integrity often result in world-changing events.

Good News

God hears and answers the prayers of those who seek to serve him.

Optional Prayer Time

Lead the group in a short prayer. Like Nehemiah did, you might acknowledge at the beginning of your prayer that God is great and deserves our praise, that God has been very kind to us, and that he will keep his promises always.

Optional Accountability Question

How can you be a more faithful servant leader in your work, with your neighbors, or at home, so that you might be more able to help others at a critical time?

DISCOVER**LIFE**

Success for the Asking

Lesson 1

Nehemiah 1:1-4

[1]The words of Nehemiah son of Hacaliah:

In the month of Kislev in the twentieth year, while I was in the citadel of Susa, [2]Hanani, one of my brothers, came from Judah with some other men, and I questioned them about the Jewish remnant that survived the exile, and also about Jerusalem.

[3]They said to me, "Those who survived the exile and are back in the province are in great trouble and disgrace. The wall of Jerusalem is broken down, and its gates have been burned with fire."

[4]When I heard these things, I sat down and wept. For some days I mourned and fasted and prayed before the God of heaven.

Nehemiah 1:5-11

Then I said:

"O LORD, God of heaven, the great and awesome God, who keeps his covenant of love with those who love him and obey his commands, [6]let your ear be attentive and your eyes open to hear the prayer your servant is praying before you day and night for your servants, the people of Israel. I confess the sins we Israelites, including myself and my father's house, have committed against you. [7]We have acted very wickedly toward you. We have not obeyed the commands, decrees and laws you gave your servant Moses.

[8]"Remember the instruction you gave your servant Moses, saying, 'If you are unfaithful, I will scatter you among the nations, [9]but if you return to me and obey my commands, then even if your exiled people are at the farthest horizon, I will gather them from there and bring them to the place I have chosen as a dwelling for my Name.'

[10]"They are your servants and your people, whom you redeemed by your great strength and your mighty hand. [11]O Lord, let your ear be attentive to the prayer of this your servant and to the prayer of your servants who delight in revering your name. Give your servant success today by granting him favor in the presence of this man."

I was cupbearer to the king.

Nehemiah 2:1-6

[1]In the month of Nisan in the twentieth year of King Artaxerxes, when wine was brought for him, I took the wine and gave it to the king. I had not been sad in his presence before; [2]so the king asked me, "Why does your face look so sad when you are not ill? This can be nothing but sadness of heart."

I was very much afraid, [3]but I said to the king, "May the king live forever! Why should my face not look sad when the city where my fathers are buried lies in ruins, and its gates have been destroyed by fire?"

[4]The king said to me, "What is it you want?"

Then I prayed to the God of heaven, [5]and I answered the king, "If it pleases the king and if your servant has found favor in his sight, let him send me to the city in Judah where my fathers are buried so that I can rebuild it."

[6]Then the king, with the queen sitting beside him, asked me, "How long will your journey take, and when will you get back?" It pleased the king to send me; so I set a time.

Nehemiah 2:7-10

[7]I also said to him, "If it pleases the king, may I have letters to the governors of Trans-Euphrates, so that they will provide me safe-conduct until I arrive in Judah? [8]And may I have a letter to Asaph, keeper of the king's forest, so he will give me timber to make beams for the gates of the citadel by the temple and for the city wall and for the residence I will occupy?" And because the gracious hand of my God was upon me, the king granted my requests. [9]So I went to the governors of Trans-Euphrates and gave them the king's letters. The king had also sent army officers and cavalry with me.

[10]When Sanballat the Horonite and Tobiah the Ammonite official heard about this, they were very much disturbed that someone had come to promote the welfare of the Israelites.

Questions

1. **If you could ask for one major change in your country or community or family, what would you ask for?**
2. **Nehemiah 1:1-4**
   a. What does Hanani report concerning Jerusalem?
   b. How does Nehemiah react to the news, and what does that tell us about him?
3. **Nehemiah 1:5-11**
   a. How does Nehemiah address God?
   b. What does Nehemiah confess?
   c. What promise does Nehemiah claim, and why?
   d. What does he ask for himself?
   e. What does a cupbearer or food taster for royalty actually do?
4. **Nehemiah 2:1-6**
   a. Would you consider Nehemiah fearful or bold? Why?
   b. How does God give Nehemiah the success he had prayed for?
   c. What insight do we gain into Nehemiah's prayer life from verse 4?
5. **Nehemiah 2:7-10**
   a. How does Nehemiah show forethought and careful planning?
   b. How does Nehemiah account for the king's consent to his request?
   c. What hostile reaction does Nehemiah encounter?

STUDIES IN THIS SERIES

afterWord

Fewer Leaders, Greater Expectations

While the pool of workers in business and industry continues to shrink, the job of the leader grows more demanding as business changes at an accelerating rate and leaders have to juggle more duties, according to William Byham, president and CEO of Development Dimensions International, a human resources and training consulting firm.

"The jump bar is going up, and there are more bars," says Byham. "We're running into it all the time in our company. We're partnering with a company and also competing with them. It gets complicated."

Mergers, acquisitions, expansions, and organizational restructurings are coming at a faster rate. Meanwhile, businesses are venturing into the global marketplace, so leaders have to be able to adjust to other cultures and transcend geographic boundaries.

"You have to be skilled in more things, and you have to be better in each of those areas," says Byham, author of a dozen books on management.

—*SMALL BUSINESS NEWS PITTSBURGH,* MARCH 2000

The Measure of Greatness

Here is how Jesus turned the power scale upside-down. Greatness is measured by taking the last place, by a total commitment to welcome the "little ones," by a breadth of sympathy and an openness to all who name his name, by a passion for personal purity, by toughness with ourselves but gentleness with others. Here are the questions he gives to measure our greatness:

Not "How many people help me?" but "How *deep* is my commitment to others?"

Not "Whom do I let into the circle of influence?" but "How *long* and *broad* is my circle of fellowship? Whom can I include and still be loyal to Jesus?"

Not "How can I best develop myself?" but "How *intense* is my passion to be pure and useful?"

—LEIGHTON FORD IN *TRANSFORMING LEADERSHIP* (INTERVARSITY PRESS)

What Will Others Think?

If Jesus Christ had taken a poll, he would never have preached the gospel.

—U.S. REP. HENRY HYDE ON ABC-TV'S "THIS WEEK" (12/13/98)

A Fresh Look at Prayer

I used to write in my daily calendar, "7:00-7:30 a.m.: Prayer." But many times I passed that up. It was one more thing to pass by that day. Now I write "7:00-7:30 a.m.: God."

Somehow that's a little harder to neglect.

—JOHN RICHES IN *CHRISTIAN SPIRITUALITY: THEMES FROM THE TRADITION* (PAULIST PRESS)

To answer prayer is God's universal rule. . . . God's Word does not say, "Call unto me, and you will thereby be trained into the happy art of knowing how to be denied. Ask, and you will learn sweet patience by getting nothing." Far from it. But it is definite, clear and positive: "Ask, and it shall be given unto you."

—E. M. BOUNDS

Success and Failure

For slightly more than thirty years Erma Bombeck wrote her humor column. During that time, she published fifteen books, was recognized as one of the twenty-five most influential women in America, appeared frequently on the television show *Good Morning America,* was featured on the cover of *Time* magazine, received innumerable honors (such as the American Cancer Society's Medal of Honor), and was awarded fifteen honorary degrees. But during that span of time, Erma Bombeck also experienced incredible troubles and trials including breast cancer, a mastectomy, and kidney failure. And she wasn't shy about sharing her perspective on her life experiences:

> I speak at college commencement, and I tell everyone I'm up here and they're down there, not because of my successes, but my failures. Then I proceed to spin all of them off—a comedy record album that sold two copies in Beirut . . . a sitcom that lasted about as long as a donut in our house . . . a Broadway play that never saw Broadway . . . a book signing where I attracted two people: one who wanted directions to the restroom and the other who wanted to buy the desk.
>
> What you have to tell yourself is, "I'm not a failure. I failed at doing something." There's a big difference. . . . Personally and career-wise, it's been a corduroy road. I've buried babies, lost parents, had cancer, and worried over kids. The trick is to put it all in perspective . . . and that's what I do for a living.

—JOHN C. MAXWELL IN *FAILING FORWARD* (THOMAS NELSON PUBLISHERS)

Focus on What Matters Most

Each morning I make a W.A.M.M. (What Activities Matter Most?) list. I need crystal clarity on what's important and what's peripheral.

Peter Drucker writes that recognizing what counts as a true contribution is the great challenge for people in work like ours. If I don't do this, it's embarrassing to me how much time I can waste.

Sloth, Frederick Beuchner said, isn't necessarily incompatible with heavy activity. It's failing to do what needs to be done when it needs to be done. Like the kamikaze pilot who flew seventeen missions.

—JOHN ORTBERG IN *LEADERSHIP*

DISCOVER*LIFE*

They Had Their Backs to a Wall

Lesson 2

1. **Do you agree or disagree with this statement: "A certain amount of opposition is a great help to a person"? Explain your answer.**

Transitional Comment

Nehemiah and those who worked with him had to face and overcome great opposition in rebuilding the wall around the city of Jerusalem.

2. **Nehemiah 2:11-13, 16**

[11]I went to Jerusalem, and after staying there three days [12]I set out during the night with a few men. I had not told anyone what my God had put in my heart to do for Jerusalem. There were no mounts with me except the one I was riding on.

[13]By night I went out through the Valley Gate toward the Jackal Well and the Dung Gate, examining the walls of Jerusalem, which had been broken down, and its gates, which had been destroyed by fire.

[16]The officials did not know where I had gone or what I was doing, because as yet I had said nothing to the Jews or the priests or nobles or officials or any others who would be doing the work.

Introductory Comment

After arriving at Jerusalem from Persia, Nehemiah ventures out to inspect the damage before challenging the leaders and people to rebuild the wall.

Questions

a. **Whose plan is it to rebuild the walls of Jerusalem (v. 12)?**

What does this tell us about God?

What does it say about Nehemiah's relationship to God?

b. **What is the first step in Nehemiah's rebuilding project?**

Why do you think he performed this inspection at night?

What did he find?

Why do you think he hid his plan from the leaders of the city for a while?

Helpful Note

- *Valley Gate, Jackal Wall, and Dung Gate.* Points along the east side of Jerusalem. The two gates were about a third of a mile apart.

3. **Nehemiah 2:17-20**

[17]Then I said to them, "You see the trouble we are in: Jerusalem lies in ruins, and its gates have been burned with fire. Come, let us rebuild the wall of Jerusalem, and we will no longer be in disgrace." [18]I also told them about the gracious hand of my God upon me and what the king had said to me.

They replied, "Let us start rebuilding." So they began this good work. [19]But when Sanballat the Horonite, Tobiah the Ammonite official and Geshem the Arab heard about it, they mocked and ridiculed us. "What is this you are doing?" they asked. "Are you rebelling against the king?"

[20]I answered them by saying, "The God of heaven will give us success. We his servants will start rebuilding, but as for you, you have no share in Jerusalem or any claim or historic right to it."

Introductory Comment

The inspection completed, Nehemiah challenges the people to rebuild the walls of Jerusalem. God wanted the wall rebuilt as a first step in reestablishing the nation from which Jesus Christ would come.

Questions

a. **What reasons does Nehemiah give for rebuilding the walls of Jerusalem?**

To whom does he address his concerns (see also v. 16)?

How do the people respond?

Why does Nehemiah use the plural pronouns "we" and "us"?

How important was it that he share his testimony of God's help and the king's approval?

b. **How do neighboring leaders try to discourage Nehemiah and the people?**

Why do you suppose they did this?

c. **Why was Nehemiah confident of success?**

Why did Nehemiah expect God's help?

What do we learn about Nehemiah from this event?

What do we learn about facing opposition?

Helpful Notes

- *Sanballat.* Governor of Samaria, a territory to the north of Jerusalem. (Sanballat and Tobiah were mentioned in session 1.)
- *Tobiah.* A Jewish official in Ammon, a territory to the east of Jerusalem.
- *Geshem.* Head of the desert tribes in northern Arabia, which lay south of Jerusalem. Jerusalem faced opposition on nearly every side.

4. **Nehemiah 4:1-6**

[1]When Sanballat heard that we were rebuilding the wall, he became angry and was greatly incensed. He ridiculed the Jews, [2]and in the presence of his associates and the army of Samaria, he said, "What are those feeble Jews doing? Will they restore their wall? Will they offer sacrifices? Will they finish in a

day? Can they bring the stones back to life from those heaps of rubble—burned as they are?"

[3]Tobiah the Ammonite, who was at his side, said, "What they are building—if even a fox climbed up on it, he would break down their wall of stones!"

[4]Hear us, O our God, for we are despised. Turn their insults back on their own heads. Give them over as plunder in a land of captivity. [5]Do not cover up their guilt or blot out their sins from your sight, for they have thrown insults in the face of the builders.

[6]So we rebuilt the wall till all of it reached half its height, for the people worked with all their heart.

Introductory Comment

Chapter 3 lists the projects involved in rebuilding the wall. It mentions forty key men who led the reconstruction of ten gates and forty-five sections of wall. However, neighboring nations continued their attempt to discourage the builders, since Israel's recovery posed a threat to their security.

Questions

a. How do Sanballat and Tobiah try to discourage the work?

What do you imagine their tone of voice to have been?

What sort of opposition is hardest for you to face: anger, insults, threats, gossip, or something else?

b. How does Nehemiah fight back?

Was this an effective way of responding? Explain.

c. How do the people respond after hearing their enemies' criticism and Nehemiah's prayer?

Helpful Notes

- *"Will they offer sacrifices?"* "Do they think they can pray the wall up?"
- *"Will they finish in a day?"* "Have they any idea how immense this project is?"
- *Do not cover up their guilt.* As in a number of the Psalms of the Bible (see Ps. 109), God's people here cry out for deliverance from enemies by asking for their enemies' downfall. Their prayer, however, acknowledges that God, rather than men, will decide matters of ultimate justice (Deut. 32:35).
- *burned.* Fire may have caused some of the limestone to crack and crumble.

5. Nehemiah 4:7-15

[7]But when Sanballat, Tobiah, the Arabs, the
Ammonites and the men of Ashdod heard that the
repairs to Jerusalem's walls had gone ahead and that
the gaps were being closed, they were very angry.
[8]They all plotted together to come and fight against
Jerusalem and stir up trouble against it. [9]But we
prayed to our God and posted a guard day and night
to meet this threat.

[10]Meanwhile, the people in Judah said, "The strength of the laborers is giving out, and there is so much rubble that we cannot rebuild the wall."

[11]Also our enemies said, "Before they know it or see us, we will be right there among them and will kill them and put an end to the work."

[12]Then the Jews who lived near them came and told us ten times over, "Wherever you turn, they will attack us."

[13]Therefore I stationed some of the people behind
the lowest points of the wall at the exposed places,
posting them by families, with their swords, spears
and bows. [14]After I looked things over, I stood up and
said to the nobles, the officials and the rest of the
people, "Don't be afraid of them. Remember the Lord,
who is great and awesome, and fight for your brothers, your sons and your daughters, your wives and
your homes." [15]When our enemies heard that we
were aware of their plot and that God had frustrated
it, we all returned to the wall, each to his own work.

Introductory Comment

The opposition intensifies, and Nehemiah is forced to set up a stronger defense.

Questions

a. Describe Nehemiah's double response to his enemies' plan (v. 9).

What does that confirm about Nehemiah?

What does this say about the relationship between work and prayer? Would one without the other have been enough? Explain.

b. What threatened the project at that point (vv. 10-12)?

What effect did Israel's enemies hope these rumors would have?

Have you ever known people who faced so many barriers that they gave up on something very important?

c. What countermoves does Nehemiah make?

Why did Nehemiah remind the people that God is great and awesome?

Why did he remind them also that they are fighting for sons, daughters, women, and so on?

What effect did this have on the builders? On their enemies?

d. How is God involved? Do you think the builders would have succeeded without God's help?

What do we have to do to secure God's help when we are facing problems?

Helpful Notes

- *Ashdod.* Capital of Philistia, a nation to the west of Jerusalem.
- *prayed . . . and posted a guard.* Often prayer and work go hand in hand. We acknowledge that nothing can

succeed without the Lord, and also acknowledge that he often uses us in fulfilling his plan.

6. **Nehemiah 4:16-22**

16 From that day on, half of my men did the work, while the other half were equipped with spears, shields, bows and armor. The officers posted themselves behind all the people of Judah 17 who were building the wall. Those who carried materials did their work with one hand and held a weapon in the other, 18 and each of the builders wore his sword at his side as he worked. But the man who sounded the trumpet stayed with me.

19 Then I said to the nobles, the officials and the rest of the people, "The work is extensive and spread out, and we are widely separated from each other along the wall. 20 Wherever you hear the sound of the trumpet, join us there. Our God will fight for us!"

21 So we continued the work with half the men holding spears, from the first light of dawn till the stars came out. 22 At that time I also said to the people, "Have every man and his helper stay inside Jerusalem at night, so they can serve us as guards by night and workmen by day."

Questions

a. **Describe the "alert plan" Nehemiah put into effect as the work continued.**

How does this plan show reliance on God?

How can we show our reliance on God as we enact our plans today?

How much dedication was required of those who participated in the alert plan?

b. **What do we learn about Nehemiah from chapter 4?**

What details tell us that Nehemiah was a servant leader?

What place did he give to God?

How did he handle opposition?

What good leadership techniques did he employ?

Main Ideas

- Nehemiah's bold plans to rebuild the wall of Jerusalem came from God.
- Nehemiah was courageous because he trusted God to keep his promises and did not allow himself to be deterred by opposition.
- Enemies were unable to stop the building because God's hand was in it.
- Nehemiah was used by God to plan the project, motivate the people, inspire trust in God, and frustrate the enemy.

Good News

God carries out his plans through faithful, trusting servants; and regardless of what the opposition says or does, God's plans will succeed.

Optional Prayer Time

Close the meeting with prayer. If you think group members are ready, consider asking them whether there is some opposition in their life now that they'd like you to pray about.

Optional Accountability Question

Identify a kind of opposition that has kept you from doing something you know you ought to do. Ask God to show you how to overcome the obstacle and to give you strength; then make a plan.

DISCOVER*LIFE*

They Had Their Backs to a Wall

Lesson 2

Nehemiah 2:11-13, 16

11I went to Jerusalem, and after staying there three days 12I set out during the night with a few men. I had not told anyone what my God had put in my heart to do for Jerusalem. There were no mounts with me except the one I was riding on.

13By night I went out through the Valley Gate toward the Jackal Well and the Dung Gate, examining the walls of Jerusalem, which had been broken down, and its gates, which had been destroyed by fire.

16The officials did not know where I had gone or what I was doing, because as yet I had said nothing to the Jews or the priests or nobles or officials or any others who would be doing the work.

Nehemiah 2:17-20

17Then I said to them, "You see the trouble we are in: Jerusalem lies in ruins, and its gates have been burned with fire. Come, let us rebuild the wall of Jerusalem, and we will no longer be in disgrace." 18I also told them about the gracious hand of my God upon me and what the king had said to me.

They replied, "Let us start rebuilding." So they began this good work. 19But when Sanballat the Horonite, Tobiah the Ammonite official and Geshem the Arab heard about it, they mocked and ridiculed us. "What is this you are doing?" they asked. "Are you rebelling against the king?"

20I answered them by saying, "The God of heaven will give us success. We his servants will start rebuilding, but as for you, you have no share in Jerusalem or any claim or historic right to it."

Nehemiah 4:1-6

1When Sanballat heard that we were rebuilding the wall, he became angry and was greatly incensed. He ridiculed the Jews, 2and in the presence of his associates and the army of Samaria, he said, "What are those feeble Jews doing? Will they restore their wall? Will they offer sacrifices? Will they finish in a day? Can they bring the stones back to life from those heaps of rubble—burned as they are?"

3Tobiah the Ammonite, who was at his side, said, "What they are building—if even a fox climbed up on it, he would break down their wall of stones!"

4Hear us, O our God, for we are despised. Turn their insults back on their own heads. Give them over as plunder in a land of captivity. 5Do not cover up their guilt or blot out their sins from your sight, for they have thrown insults in the face of the builders.

6So we rebuilt the wall till all of it reached half its height, for the people worked with all their heart.

Nehemiah 4:7-15

7But when Sanballat, Tobiah, the Arabs, the Ammonites and the men of Ashdod heard that the repairs to Jerusalem's walls had gone ahead and that the gaps were being closed, they were very angry. 8They all plotted together to come and fight against Jerusalem and stir up trouble against it. 9But we prayed to our God and posted a guard day and night to meet this threat.

10Meanwhile, the people in Judah said, "The strength of the laborers is giving out, and there is so much rubble that we cannot rebuild the wall."

11Also our enemies said, "Before they know it or see us, we will be right there among them and will kill them and put an end to the work."

12Then the Jews who lived near them came and told us ten times over, "Wherever you turn, they will attack us."

13Therefore I stationed some of the people behind the lowest points of the wall at the exposed places, posting them by families, with their swords, spears and bows. 14After I looked things over, I stood up and said to the nobles, the officials and the rest of the people, "Don't be afraid of them. Remember the Lord, who is great and awesome, and fight for your brothers, your sons and your daughters, your wives and your homes." 15When our enemies heard that we were aware of their plot and that God had frustrated it, we all returned to the wall, each to his own work.

Nehemiah 4:16-22

16From that day on, half of my men did the work, while the other half were equipped with spears, shields, bows and armor. The officers posted themselves behind all the people of Judah 17who were building the wall. Those who carried materials did their work with one hand and held a weapon in the other, 18and each of the builders wore his sword at his side as he worked. But the man who sounded the trumpet stayed with me.

19Then I said to the nobles, the officials and the rest of the people, "The work is extensive and spread out, and we are widely separated from each other along the wall. 20Wherever you hear the sound of the trumpet, join us there. Our God will fight for us!"

21So we continued the work with half the men holding spears, from the first light of dawn till the stars came out. 22At that time I also said to the people, "Have every man and his helper stay inside Jerusalem at night, so they can serve us as guards by night and workmen by day."

Questions

1. **Do you agree or disagree with this statement: "A certain amount of opposition is a great help to a man"? Explain your answer.**

2. **Nehemiah 2:11-13, 16**
   a. Whose plan is it to rebuild the walls of Jerusalem (v. 12)?
   b. What is the first step in Nehemiah's rebuilding project?

(continued on next page)

STUDIES IN THIS SERIES

3. Nehemiah 2:17-20

a. What reasons does Nehemiah give for rebuilding the walls of Jerusalem?

b. How do neighboring leaders try to discourage Nehemiah and the people?

c. Why was Nehemiah confident of success?

4. Nehemiah 4:1-6

a. How do Sanballat and Tobiah try to discourage the work?

b. How does Nehemiah fight back?

c. How do the people respond after hearing their enemies' criticism and Nehemiah's prayer?

5. Nehemiah 4:7-15

a. Describe Nehemiah's double response to his enemies' plan (v. 9).

b. What threatened the project at that point (vv. 10-12)?

c. What countermoves does Nehemiah make?

d. How is God involved? Do you think the builders would have succeeded without God's help?

6. Nehemiah 4:16-22

a. Describe the "alert plan" Nehemiah put into effect as the work continued.

b. What do we learn about Nehemiah from chapter 4?

*after*Word

God's Will for My Life

Early in my college experience I was praying about God's will for my life. In a flash I saw the future laid out before me: I would transfer from my secular college to Moody Bible Institute and study for the ministry. I would also marry the girl I was dating.

Thrilled at the prospect, I began to praise the Lord. The plan was perfect—with one exception. No one seemed to have informed Moody Bible Institute. A few months after submitting my application, I received a polite letter of rejection. The girl I was "supposed" to marry soon transferred to another school and began dating someone else.

God is infallible in all he says or does and never makes an error in judgment. The same cannot be said of us. We must test any sense of prompting we feel by the clear teaching of God's Word. The Scriptures are always the foundation in matters of guidance and should never be overruled by other sources. God will never prompt us to act contrary to his Word.

Yet many of the decisions we make involve choices between options clearly within the bounds of God's Word. In such cases, being "led of the Spirit" may not be a matter of deciding whom we should marry or which job we should take, as much as one of recognizing the potential for Spirit-empowered obedience to the clear directives of God's Word. How we act once we have made the choice between two equally sanctioned options is often more important than the choice itself.

Certainly, God is concerned about the everyday decisions we must make. He cares about our decision to work at McDonalds over Burger King, or our choice of marrying Jane rather than Joan. But when Romans 8:14 speaks of being "led by the Spirit of God," it refers to our responsibility to put to death the old nature and walk in the new nature (see Rom. 8:13-14). When Paul speaks of being "led" by the Spirit and "keeping in step" with the Spirit, he is calling believers to demonstrate the fruit of the spirit instead of indulging in the deeds of the flesh (Gal. 5:18, 23-25).

Our opportunities to say "no" to the flesh and "yes" to the Spirit may not be as glamorous as the kind of decisions we usually associate with divine guidance, but they happen every day. They are reflected in a mother's choice to forgive rather than hold on to bitterness when she is hurt by one of her family members. An employee chooses the path marked out by God's Spirit when he refuses to engage in workplace gossip. A church member is being led by the Spirit when he notices someone struggling with sin and uses God's Word to restore him (see Gal. 6:1).

—JOHN KOESSLER IN *MOODY*, MARCH/APRIL 2000

Courage

Give us grace, O God, to do the deed which we well know cries out to be done. Let us not hesitate because of ease, or the words of men's mouths, or our own lives. Mighty causes are calling us. . . . But they call with voices that mean work and sacrifice and death. Mercifully grant us, O God, the spirit of Esther, that we say, "I will go unto the King, and if I perish, I perish." Amen.

—W. E. B. DUBOIS, A FOUNDER OF THE NAACP

The truth of the matter is that you always know the right thing to do. The hard part is doing it.

—GEN. H. NORMAN SCHWARZKOPF

Prayer Is Work

Prayer is not the foe of work, it does not paralyze activity. It works mightily. . . . It springs activity, stimulates desire and effort. Prayer is not an opiate but a tonic, it does not lull to sleep but arouses anew for action. The lazy man does not, will not, cannot pray, for prayer demands energy.

—E. M. BOUNDS

How to Be Good and Mad

Lesson 3

1. When is it OK to be angry?

What are some things we should probably be angry about?

What purposes can healthy anger serve?

Transitional Comment

Nehemiah got angry for the right reasons. He acted to correct a situation that displeased God.

2. Nehemiah 5:1-5

[1]Now the men and their wives raised a great outcry against their Jewish brothers. [2]Some were saying, "We and our sons and daughters are numerous; in order for us to eat and stay alive, we must get grain."

[3]Others were saying, "We are mortgaging our fields, our vineyards and our homes to get grain during the famine."

[4]Still others were saying, "We have had to borrow money to pay the king's tax on our fields and vineyards. [5]Although we are of the same flesh and blood as our countrymen and though our sons are as good as theirs, yet we have to subject our sons and daughters to slavery. Some of our daughters have already been enslaved, but we are powerless, because our fields and our vineyards belong to others."

Introductory Comment

When social and economic injustice make life extremely hard for the people, Nehemiah listens and acts quickly to correct the problem.

Questions

a. What problems among the Jews trigger an outcry?

From whom did the complaints come?

Whom were the complaints against?

b. What are the underlying causes of the problem?

Who contributed to the problem?

What was unjust about the situation?

How do you usually respond when you are a victim of societal injustice?

Helpful Notes

- *famine.* Famine was common in Palestine. Sometimes it was the direct result of the disobedience of God's people.
- *the tax.* Severe taxes levied on conquered people by the Persian king.
- *subjected to slavery.* Poor families borrowed money by using family members as security. Failing to repay the loan, however, meant that family members could be sold into servanthood.

3. Nehemiah 5:6-11

[6]When I heard their outcry and these charges, I was very angry. [7]I pondered them in my mind and then accused the nobles and officials. I told them, "You are exacting usury from your own countrymen!" So I called together a large meeting to deal with them [8]and said: "As far as possible, we have bought back our Jewish brothers who were sold to the Gentiles. Now you are selling your brothers, only for them to be sold back to us!" They kept quiet, because they could find nothing to say.

[9]So I continued, "What you are doing is not right. Shouldn't you walk in the fear of our God to avoid the reproach of our Gentile enemies? [10]I and my brothers and my men are also lending the people money and grain. But let the exacting of usury stop! [11]Give back to them immediately their fields, vineyards, olive groves and houses, and also the usury you are charging them—the hundredth part of the money, grain, new wine and oil."

Questions

a. How does Nehemiah respond to this outcry?

Was his anger justified?

What does Nehemiah's anger tell us about him?

b. After considering the issue, who does Nehemiah say is the source of the problems?

What charges did he lodge against the officials?

What does their response (v. 8) tell us?

How do you react when you are accused of something of which you are guilty?

Why are leaders usually given more blame?

c. What solution does Nehemiah propose?

What motives did he appeal to (v. 9)?

How did Nehemiah practice what he preached?

In what way did the proposed solution seem to go beyond simple justice?

How easy is it for you to give more than you are required to?

Helpful Notes

- *usury.* Lending money for interest—a practice forbidden by Old Testament law (Lev. 25:25-37).
- *selling your brothers.* This was also against Old Testament law (Lev. 25:39-43).
- *fear of the Lord.* Respect for God and his standards for life.
- *avoid the reproach of our Gentile enemies.* The Israelite practice of usury brought them into disgrace in the eyes of their neighbors, and tarnished the name of the true God among the nations.
- *the hundredth part.* Probably a monthly interest rate of one percent.

4. Nehemiah 5:12-13

[12]"We will give it back," they said. "And we will not demand anything more from them. We will do as you say."

Then I summoned the priests and made the nobles and officials take an oath to do what they had promised. [13]I also shook out the folds of my robe and said, "In this way may God shake out of his house and possessions every man who does not keep this promise. So may such a man be shaken out and emptied!"

At this the whole assembly said, "Amen," and praised the LORD. And the people did as they had promised.

Questions

a. **What do the nobles and officials do to correct the situation?**

Why do you think Nehemiah called everyone to make their promise publicly?

Why is promise-keeping important to society?

b. **What was the point of the oath?**

What impact did Nehemiah intend his symbolic action (v. 13) to have?

Whom did the people praise for correcting the injustice (v. 13b)?

Helpful Notes

- *shook out the folds of my robe.* The folds of a robe were used to carry loose grain and the like. A person simply grasped the robe below the belt and lifted it up to form a pocket. Kernels of grain that stuck to the robe after it was emptied would be shaken out.
- *Amen.* "So let it be."

5. Nehemiah 5:14-19

[14]Moreover, from the twentieth year of King Artaxerxes, when I was appointed to be their governor in the land of Judah, until his thirty-second year—twelve years—neither I nor my brothers ate the food allotted to the governor. [15]But the earlier governors—those preceding me—placed a heavy burden on the people and took forty shekels of silver from them in addition to food and wine. Their assistants also lorded it over the people. But out of reverence for God I did not act like that. [16]Instead, I devoted myself to the work on this wall. All my men were assembled there for the work; we did not acquire any land.

[17]Furthermore, a hundred and fifty Jews and officials ate at my table, as well as those who came to us from the surrounding nations. [18]Each day one ox, six choice sheep and some poultry were prepared for me, and every ten days an abundant supply of wine of all kinds. In spite of all this, I never demanded the food allotted to the governor, because the demands were heavy on these people.

[19]Remember me with favor, O my God, for all I have done for these people.

Introductory Comment

Nehemiah set a good example of a responsible public official in a situation where his subjects were poor and stretched to the limit.

Questions

a. **Compare Nehemiah's style of leadership with those who preceded him.**

Why did he act this way?

For what reason did Nehemiah give up his food allowance?

Tell of a time when you gave up something you had a right to have, in order to help others.

b. **If Nehemiah had led like the governors before him, how might the nation's situation have been different?**

What attitudes and actions make for good government officials today?

c. **What evidence is there in this chapter that God cared for the oppressed people?**

Summarize what God did through Nehemiah to lift the people's burden.

Does God still care when people are burdened? Explain.

Helpful Notes

- *the food allotted.* A ruler had the right to demand from the people food for his table.

Main Ideas

- Hearing of the terrible oppression among his people, Nehemiah targeted the leading oppressors and demanded that they right the wrongs.
- Nehemiah practiced what he preached and used his own resources to help others.
- While there will always be problems in a nation, people who exercise God-given principles of leadership can make the difference between a nation that is growing toward greatness and a nation that is degenerating into chaos.

Good News

God hates evil and injustice; he stands up for those who are oppressed.

Optional Prayer Time

Ask a few of the group members ahead of time if they would lead in prayer at the close of the meeting.

Optional Accountability Question

Think of something you have an abundance of—something that could be of great value to others if you shared it with them. Between now and next week, will you give that away so that others might be blessed?

DISCOVER*LIFE*

How to Be Good and Mad

Lesson 3

Nehemiah 5:1-5

1 Now the men and their wives
raised a great outcry against their
Jewish brothers. 2 Some were saying,
"We and our sons and daughters are
numerous; in order for us to eat and
stay alive, we must get grain."

3 Others were saying, "We are
mortgaging our fields, our vineyards
and our homes to get grain during
the famine."

4 Still others were saying, "We have
had to borrow money to pay the
king's tax on our fields and vine-
yards. 5 Although we are of the same
flesh and blood as our countrymen
and though our sons are as good as
theirs, yet we have to subject our sons
and daughters to slavery. Some of our
daughters have already been en-
slaved, but we are powerless, because
our fields and our vineyards belong
to others."

Nehemiah 5:6-11

6 When I heard their outcry and
these charges, I was very angry. 7 I
pondered them in my mind and then
accused the nobles and officials. I
told them, "You are exacting usury
from your own countrymen!" So I
called together a large meeting to
deal with them 8 and said: "As far as
possible, we have bought back our
Jewish brothers who were sold to the
Gentiles. Now you are selling your
brothers, only for them to be sold
back to us!" They kept quiet, because
they could find nothing to say.

9 So I continued, "What you are
doing is not right. Shouldn't you
walk in the fear of our God to avoid
the reproach of our Gentile enemies?
10 I and my brothers and my men are
also lending the people money and
grain. But let the exacting of usury
stop! 11 Give back to them immedi-
ately their fields, vineyards, olive
groves and houses, and also the
usury you are charging them—the
hundredth part of the money, grain,
new wine and oil."

Nehemiah 5:12-13

12 "We will give it back," they said.
"And we will not demand anything
more from them. We will do as you
say."

Then I summoned the priests and
made the nobles and officials take an
oath to do what they had promised.
13 I also shook out the folds of my robe
and said, "In this way may God
shake out of his house and posses-
sions every man who does not keep
this promise. So may such a man be
shaken out and emptied!"

At this the whole assembly said,
"Amen," and praised the LORD. And
the people did as they had promised.

Nehemiah 5:14-19

14 Moreover, from the twentieth
year of King Artaxerxes, when I was
appointed to be their governor in the
land of Judah, until his thirty-second
year—twelve years—neither I nor
my brothers ate the food allotted to
the governor. 15 But the earlier gover-
nors—those preceding me—placed a
heavy burden on the people and took
forty shekels of silver from them in
addition to food and wine. Their
assistants also lorded it over the peo-
ple. But out of reverence for God I
did not act like that. 16 Instead, I
devoted myself to the work on this
wall. All my men were assembled
there for the work; we did not
acquire any land.

17 Furthermore, a hundred and
fifty Jews and officials ate at my table,
as well as those who came to us from
the surrounding nations. 18 Each day
one ox, six choice sheep and some
poultry were prepared for me, and
every ten days an abundant supply of
wine of all kinds. In spite of all this, I
never demanded the food allotted to
the governor, because the demands
were heavy on these people.

19 Remember me with favor, O my
God, for all I have done for these peo-
ple.

Questions

1. When is it OK to be angry?

2. Nehemiah 5:1-5

a. What problems among the Jews trigger an outcry?

b. What are the underlying causes of the problem?

3. Nehemiah 5:6-11

a. How does Nehemiah respond to this outcry?

b. After considering the issue, who does Nehemiah say is the source of the problems?

c. What solution does Nehemiah propose?

4. Nehemiah 5:12-13

a. What do the nobles and officials do to correct the situation?

b. What was the point of the oath?

5. Nehemiah 5:14-19

a. Compare Nehemiah's style of leadership with those who preceded him.

b. If Nehemiah had led like the governors before him, how might the nation's situation have been different?

c. What evidence is there in this chapter that God cared for the oppressed people?

STUDIES IN THIS SERIES

afterWord

Answering the Critics

Mike, one of our elders, suggested that we put on paper all the criticisms we had heard and address them head on. We listed all the questions and accusations that we could think of, including the ones we deemed ridiculous. Had we asked people to leave the church? Was the leadership team power hungry? Was the pastor doing the thinking for the elder board? Were we against charismatics?

Since we were only days away from our annual congregational meeting, we decided to make time on the agenda for the list of questions—with answers.

I started the meeting with a nervous stomach. "Most of you know that some families have recently left our church. (I listed their names.) You have heard stories which have likely raised serious questions in your mind. You may have assumed that since we have made no public statement that everything is secret, but this is not the case. This evening I want to discuss openly concerns that may be on your hearts."

There was dead silence in the room. As I proceeded down the list of concerns and criticisms, I could tell people were on board, although they were surprised at our candor. As I continued, people began to relax and sit deeper into their seats. Smiles broke out at some of the questions. When finished, I held my breath, prayed to myself, then asked if there were any additional questions. I wondered if a dam of accusations would break out. Again, there was silence. A peaceful silence.

At the end of the meeting, many people came forward to affirm the leaders for being forthright. I went to bed that evening knowing that a possible division in the congregation in the congregation had been put to rest. Time has proven us right. And trust in our leadership team has increased.

—LANNY KILGORE IN *LEADERSHIP*, SPRING 2000

He Did One Thing Well

Once renowned evangelist Dwight L. Moody entered into a personal relationship with the Lord Jesus Christ, he increasingly became committed—some said obsessively committed—to fulfilling the Great Commission. Indeed, when he overheard the British evangelist Henry Varley say that the world has yet "to see what the Lord can do with a man wholly consecrated to Christ," Moody determined to be that man. He allowed nothing to stand in the way.

Because the drive to rescue lost souls and equip a new generation of Christian workers was so strong in Moody, he made every imaginable effort to avoid getting bogged down in secondary issues.

Like effective evangelists throughout history, this Massachusetts-born preacher refused to take sides on divisive doctrines such as God's sovereignty versus human responsibility, or any one of a host of other issues that mark various denominations.

No one could draw Moody into debates over the merits of one mode of baptism over another. This charitable seeker of lost souls always advocated ministering with people of all denominations as long as they professed love for the Lord Jesus Christ and exhibited a desire to make Him known.

—LYLE W. DORSETT IN *MOODY*, NOVEMBER/DECEMBER 1999

Leaders, Lose the Ego

The real power of leadership lies in servanthood. Damien, the missionary to the lepers of Hawaii, had no resources to speak of, yet he appeared rich. He committed himself to the malformed and dying. In those he served, he wakened an ability to transcend themselves. His selflessness caused the hopeless to care less about their own suffering than they did about the needs of others. Damien gave such dignity to the dying that he brought the word *hope* back to their vocabulary. He proved that servant leadership is never a saucer where surface and depth lie close together. Leadership is rather a well where the substance of the soul lies deep and its well rope is long to reach the cold, pure depths.

What denotes servant leadership? A strange unawareness of ego. Servant leaders are task-centered. Because they tend to pick great tasks, they always feel overwhelmed and inadequate. Because they feel inadequate, they seek to look beyond themselves for answers. They don't do this to be heroic. They do it to be honest. They know they don't have all the answers.

Their commitment to the task means that real leaders . . . know that hiring strong associates helps them eliminate the weaknesses in their organization. Strong organizations are more important to them than egoistic reputations. They crave a strong organization above a good image. They deplore incompetency, even when incompetents by contrast point up their strengths. Their feeling of weakness has a wonderful spiritual dimension. Feelings of inadequacy in Christian leaders cause them to compensate for their weaknesses by turning inwardly to Christ.

—CALVIN MILLER IN *THE EMPOWERED LEADER* (BROADMAN & HOLMAN PUBLISHERS, 1995)

Servant Leadership

Biblical servant leadership has paradoxical qualities. Leaders have the courage to make decisions on behalf of the group, when group well-being is endangered. But the leadership privileges normally associated with status, ego, financial gain, and a lust for power have been replaced by servanthood attitudes.

—STAN PLETT

DISCOVER*LIFE*

When Push Comes to Shove

Lesson 4

1. **What is the best thing a person can do when facing a danger or threat?**

   What is your first response to danger?

   Has your response to danger changed as you grow older?

Transitional Comment

Nehemiah faced many dangers and threats, and he handled them amazingly well.

2. **Nehemiah 6:1-4**

[1]When word came to Sanballat, Tobiah, Geshem the Arab and the rest of our enemies that I had rebuilt the wall and not a gap was left in it—though up to that time I had not set the doors in the gates—
[2]Sanballat and Geshem sent me this message: "Come, let us meet together in one of the villages on the plain of Ono."

But they were scheming to harm me; [3]so I sent messengers to them with this reply: "I am carrying on a great project and cannot go down. Why should the work stop while I leave it and go down to you?"
[4]Four times they sent me the same message, and each time I gave them the same answer.

Introductory Comment

Having failed to stop Nehemiah and the builders with threats, Sanballat and other enemies plot against Nehemiah's life.

Questions

a. **What new tactics do Nehemiah's enemies try?**

   What seems to have been their intent?

   Why were they so persistent?

   Why are some salespeople notorious for being persistent?

b. **What keeps Nehemiah from being lured into their trap?**

   How did Nehemiah respond to his enemies?

   What does Nehemiah's response reveal about his leadership?

   How can focusing clearly on God-given goals help us decide how to use our time?

Helpful Notes

- *Sanballat, Tobiah, Geshem.* Leaders of territories surrounding Jerusalem. (See notes on Neh. 2:17-20 in lesson 2.)
- *plain of Ono.* Located about twenty miles northwest of Jerusalem, it was more than a day's journey for Nehemiah.

3. **Nehemiah 6:5-9**

[5]Then, the fifth time, Sanballat sent his aide to me with the same message, and in his hand was an unsealed letter [6]in which was written:

"It is reported among the nations—and Geshem says it is true—that you and the Jews are plotting to revolt, and therefore you are building the wall. Moreover, according to these reports you are about to become their king [7]and have even appointed prophets to make this proclamation about you in Jerusalem: 'There is a king in Judah!' Now this report will get back to the king; so come, let us confer together."

[8]I sent him this reply: "Nothing like what you are saying is happening; you are just making it up out of your head."

[9]They were all trying to frighten us, thinking, "Their hands will get too weak for the work, and it will not be completed."

[But I prayed,] "Now strengthen my hands."

Questions

a. **Why might Sanballat have left the letter unsealed?**

   Why do you think he added "Now this report will get back to the king"?

   What obvious rumors are evident in Sanballat's letter?

   What are the dangers of accepting rumors as true?

b. **What is the gist of Nehemiah's reply to Sanballat?**

   How did he counter Sanballat's fear tactics?

   How can we combat fear?

c. **Where does Nehemiah get his courage?**

   How can we find strength in difficult moments?

Helpful Notes

- *unsealed letter.* Sanballat no doubt left the letter unsealed so that everyone could read its contents and spread the rumors.
- *It is reported.* A malicious rumor, containing exaggerated and inaccurate information. Note that, as with most rumors, no original source of the information is given.
- *their king.* Persian rulers allowed no kings to rule over the peoples they conquered.

4. **Nehemiah 6:10-14**

[10]One day I went to the house of Shemaiah son of Delaiah, the son of Mehetabel, who was shut in at his home. He said, "Let us meet in the house of God, inside the temple, and let us close the temple doors,

because men are coming to kill you—by night they are coming to kill you."

[11]But I said, "Should a man like me run away? Or should one like me go into the temple to save his life? I will not go!" [12]I realized that God had not sent him, but that he had prophesied against me because Tobiah and Sanballat had hired him. [13]He had been hired to intimidate me so that I would commit a sin by doing this, and then they would give me a bad name to discredit me.

[14]Remember Tobiah and Sanballat, O my God, because of what they have done; remember also the prophetess Noadiah and the rest of the prophets who have been trying to intimidate me.

Introductory Comment

Having failed to harm, discredit, or frighten Nehemiah so far, Tobiah and Sanballat try still another tactic.

Questions

a. How does Shemaiah try to ensnare Nehemiah?

What would Nehemiah have lost had he given in to fear?

What would have happened to the project?

Why did the ploy fail?

b. How does Nehemiah respond to Shemaiah's tactics?

c. What does Nehemiah's response reveal about his character?

How did Nehemiah's gift of discernment help him in this situation?

Nehemiah was evidently not concerned about his life; what was he concerned about (v. 13)?

d. What does Nehemiah ask of God?

Why do you think he asked this?

Helpful Notes

- *Shemaiah.* Possibly a priest of the temple, and a friend of Tobiah and Sanballat. Acted as an enemy agent (v. 12).
- *inside the temple.* Not being a priest, Nehemiah was forbidden by law to enter the sanctuary. The "prophet" thus tempted Nehemiah to save his life by breaking God's law, something that could have been used to discredit him as a leader. Nehemiah recognized this ploy, at least in part because no true prophet of God could give a message that contradicted God's law.
- *prophetess Noadiah.* Apparently a false prophetess who pretended to speak for God.
- *remember.* Judge them for their wrongdoing, for the saving of God's people and the preserving of God's reputation.

5. Nehemiah 6:15-19

[15]So the wall was completed on the twenty-fifth of Elul, in fifty-two days. [16]When all our enemies heard about this, all the surrounding nations were afraid and lost their self-confidence, because they realized that this work had been done with the help of our God.

[17]Also, in those days the nobles of Judah were sending many letters to Tobiah, and replies from Tobiah kept coming to them. [18]For many in Judah were under oath to him, since he was son-in-law to Shecaniah son of Arah, and his son Jehohanan had married the daughter of Meshullam son of Berekiah. [19]Moreover, they kept reporting to me his good deeds and then telling him what I said. And Tobiah sent letters to intimidate me.

Questions

a. How was such a gigantic task completed in such a short time, despite troubles from without and within?

What did God use in his plan to rebuild the wall? Consider such things as Nehemiah's leadership, his division of labor (ch. 3), the people's commitment (4:6), freedom and justice (3:11-12), and faith (2:20; 4:9, 14, 20; 6:9).

b. How do the surrounding nations respond to the news that the wall has been completed?

What did they recognize as key to the project's success?

What did they begin to realize about God?

What is the key to a strong church?

c. What problems continue to plague Nehemiah after the wall is finished?

Considering your own workplace, church, or family, which problems do you find the most difficult—problems from without or problems from within? Why?

Helpful Notes

- *Ellul.* August-September.
- *fifty-two days.* During this time the people built a basic structure that was later strengthened and extended.
- *Tobiah.* He was connected to an influential priestly family in Judah.

6. Nehemiah 7:1-3

[1]After the wall had been rebuilt and I had set the doors in place, the gatekeepers and the singers and the Levites were appointed. [2]I put in charge of Jerusalem my brother Hanani, along with Hananiah the commander of the citadel, because he was a man of integrity and feared God more than most men do. [3]I said to them, "The gates of Jerusalem are not to be opened until the sun is hot. While the gatekeepers are still on duty, have them shut the doors and bar them. Also appoint residents of Jerusalem as guards, some at their posts and some near their own houses."

Introductory Comment

With the wall completed, there still were many tasks and challenges facing Nehemiah.

Questions

a. **What three groups are first appointed after the wall is completed?**

Why do you think these groups were important?

What do they tell us about the purpose of the city?

b. **Who is put in charge?**

Where have we met Hanani before?

What qualified Hananiah for leadership?

What qualities do you look for in someone to help you at a critical time?

c. **What instructions does Nehemiah give?**

Why might he have given these instructions?

Helpful Notes

- *singers.* Choirs for temple worship.
- *Levites.* Assistants in temple worship.
- *Hanani.* Had originally brought Nehemiah the news of Jerusalem's distressing condition (Neh. 1:2).
- *until the sun is hot.* Opening the gates was delayed until mid-morning to prevent enemy attack early in the morning while people were still in bed.

Main Ideas

- Enemies attempted to stop the building of the wall with personal attacks on Nehemiah.
- Nehemiah refused to be sidetracked, deceived, or intimidated.
- The walls of Jerusalem were completed in a short amount of time with God's empowering.
- When God's people keep their focus on him through internal and external trials, even their enemies recognize God's power at work.

Good News

If God is for us, no one can be against us.

Optional Prayer Time

Like Nehemiah, even the best of people face serious trials. Ask group members if any of them wish to share a trial they are facing in which they could use God's help. Tell them you will lead in prayer about these things (and, as a leader, keep these things in your prayers through the coming week).

Optional Accountability Question

In your everyday life, do you spend more time focusing on God's plan or worrying about your own plans? Do you spend more energy on your family's physical safety than you do on their spiritual health? What about your life needs to change in this area?

DISCOVER***LIFE***

When Push Comes to Shove

Lesson 4

Nehemiah 6:1-4

[1]When word came to Sanballat, Tobiah, Geshem the Arab and the rest of our enemies that I had rebuilt the wall and not a gap was left in it—though up to that time I had not set the doors in the gates—[2]Sanballat and Geshem sent me this message: "Come, let us meet together in one of the villages on the plain of Ono."

But they were scheming to harm me; [3]so I sent messengers to them with this reply: "I am carrying on a great project and cannot go down. Why should the work stop while I leave it and go down to you?" [4]Four times they sent me the same message, and each time I gave them the same answer.

Nehemiah 6:5-9

[5]Then, the fifth time, Sanballat sent his aide to me with the same message, and in his hand was an unsealed letter [6]in which was written:

"It is reported among the nations—and Geshem says it is true—that you and the Jews are plotting to revolt, and therefore you are building the wall. Moreover, according to these reports you are about to become their king [7]and have even appointed prophets to make this proclamation about you in Jerusalem: 'There is a king in Judah!' Now this report will get back to the king; so come, let us confer together."

[8]I sent him this reply: "Nothing like what you are saying is happening; you are just making it up out of your head."

[9]They were all trying to frighten us, thinking, "Their hands will get too weak for the work, and it will not be completed."

[But I prayed,] "Now strengthen my hands."

Nehemiah 6:10-14

[10]One day I went to the house of Shemaiah son of Delaiah, the son of Mehetabel, who was shut in at his home. He said, "Let us meet in the house of God, inside the temple, and let us close the temple doors, because men are coming to kill you—by night they are coming to kill you."

[11]But I said, "Should a man like me run away? Or should one like me go into the temple to save his life? I will not go!" [12]I realized that God had not sent him, but that he had prophesied against me because Tobiah and Sanballat had hired him. [13]He had been hired to intimidate me so that I would commit a sin by doing this, and then they would give me a bad name to discredit me.

[14]Remember Tobiah and Sanballat, O my God, because of what they have done; remember also the prophetess Noadiah and the rest of the prophets who have been trying to intimidate me.

Nehemiah 6:15-19

[15]So the wall was completed on the twenty-fifth of Elul, in fifty-two days. [16]When all our enemies heard about this, all the surrounding nations were afraid and lost their self-confidence, because they realized that this work had been done with the help of our God.

[17]Also, in those days the nobles of Judah were sending many letters to Tobiah, and replies from Tobiah kept coming to them. [18]For many in Judah were under oath to him, since he was son-in-law to Shecaniah son of Arah, and his son Jehohanan had married the daughter of Meshullam son of Berekiah. [19]Moreover, they kept reporting to me his good deeds and then telling him what I said. And Tobiah sent letters to intimidate me.

Nehemiah 7:1-3

[1]After the wall had been rebuilt and I had set the doors in place, the gatekeepers and the singers and the Levites were appointed. [2]I put in charge of Jerusalem my brother Hanani, along with Hananiah the commander of the citadel, because he was a man of integrity and feared God more than most men do. [3]I said to them, "The gates of Jerusalem are not to be opened until the sun is hot. While the gatekeepers are still on duty, have them shut the doors and bar them. Also appoint residents of Jerusalem as guards, some at their posts and some near their own houses."

STUDIES IN THIS SERIES

Lesson 1: Success for the Asking
Lesson 2: They Had Their Backs to a Wall
Lesson 3: How to be Good and Mad
Lesson 4: When Push Comes to Shove
Lesson 5: They Found Joy in a Book
Lesson 6: God Gives His People Joy
Lesson 7: The Danger of Compromise

Questions

1. **What is the best thing a person can do when facing a danger or threat?**
2. **Nehemiah 6:1-4**
   a. What new tactics do Nehemiah's enemies try?
   b. What keeps Nehemiah from being lured into their trap?
3. **Nehemiah 6:5-9**
   a. Why might Sanballat have left the letter unsealed?
   b. What is the gist of Nehemiah's reply to Sanballat?
   c. Where does Nehemiah get his courage?
4. **Nehemiah 6:10-14**
   a. How does Shemaiah try to ensnare Nehemiah?
   b. How does Nehemiah respond to Shemaiah's tactics?
   c. What does Nehemiah's response reveal about his character?
   d. What does Nehemiah ask of God?
5. **Nehemiah 6:15-19**
   a. How was such a gigantic task completed in such a short time, despite troubles from without and within?
   b. How do the surrounding nations respond to the news that the wall has been completed?
   c. What problems continue to plague Nehemiah after the wall is finished?
6. **Nehemiah 7:1-3**
   a. What three groups are first appointed after the wall is completed?
   b. Who is put in charge?
   c. What instructions does Nehemiah give?

afterWord

Keeping the Right Focus

During construction of Emerson Hall at Harvard University, president Charles Eliot invited psychologist and philosopher William James to suggest a suitable inscription for the stone lintel over the doors of the new home of the philosophy department.

After some reflection, James sent Eliot a line from the Greek philosopher Protagoras: "Man is the measure of all things."

James never heard back from Eliot, so his curiosity was piqued when he spotted artisans working on a scaffold hidden by a canvas. One morning, the scaffold and canvas were gone. The inscription? "What is man that thou art mindful of him?"

Eliot had replaced James's suggestion with words from the Psalmist. Between these two lines lies the great distance between the God-centered and the human-centered points of view.

—WARREN BIRD IN *LEADERSHIP*, SPRING 1997

Keeping Perspective

Failure is an inside job. So is success. If you want to achieve, you have to win the war in your thinking first. You can't let the failure outside you get inside you. You certainly can't control the length of your life—but you can control its width and depth. You can't control the contour of your face—but you can control its expression. You can't control the weather—but you can control the atmosphere of your mind. Why worry about things you can't control when you can keep yourself busy controlling the things that depend on you?

I read an article that highlighted the strength, courage, and resilience of the Norwegian people. Some of the toughest explorers in history have come from Norway. . . . It doesn't matter how harsh the climate or how difficult the circumstances; they always seem to persevere.

That ability has become a part of their culture. They are a nation of outdoor enthusiasts—living on the edge of the Arctic Circle. The Norwegians have a saying that I think captures their attitude: "There is no such thing as bad weather, only bad clothing."

—JOHN C. MAXWELL IN *FAILING FORWARD* (THOMAS NELSON, 2000)

> A man is not defeated by his opponents but by himself.
>
> —JAN CHRISTIAAN SMUTS

Never, Never, Never Give Up

As a young teenager, Sir Winston Churchill attended a public school called Harrow. He was a rambunctious sort and probably would have been expelled had he not been the son of the famed Lord Randolph Churchill. But Sir Winston went on to build a brilliant career in the British military, finally becoming prime minister, leading his nation through the dark days of World War II.

When asked to speak at his old school, Churchill agreed. The schoolmaster gave the prime minister a glowing introduction. The students listened intently to hear what wisdom the greatest leader in their nation would give them. Drawing himself up to his full stature—all five feet, five inches, and 235 pounds of him—Churchill made this brief but unforgettable speech: "Young men, never give up. Never give up! Never give up!! Never, never, never, never!"

How to Handle the Critics

Abraham Lincoln might have broken under the strain of the Civil War if he hadn't learned the folly of trying to answer all the angry criticism hurled at him. His description of how he handled his critics has become a literary gem.

General MacArthur had a copy of it hanging above his headquarters desk during the war; and Winston Churchill kept a framed copy of it on the walls of his study at Chartwell. It goes like this:

"If I were to try to read, much less to answer, all the attacks made on me, this shop might as well be closed for any other business. I do the very best I know how—the very best I can; and I mean to keep on doing so until the end. If the end brings me out all right, then what is said against me won't matter. If the end brings me out wrong, then ten angels swearing I was right would make no difference."

How to Run with Patience

Bob Wieland finally crossed the finish line on Thursday, November 6, 1986, the New York City Marathon's 19,413th and final finisher . . . and the first to run a marathon with his arms instead of his legs! Wieland is a 40-year-old Californian whose legs were blown off in a Vietnam battlefield. He recorded what race officials said was the slowest time in marathon history: four days, two hours, 48 minutes, 17 seconds. But he was greeted like a champion by race director Fred Lebow, who had written Wieland off as a dropout.

When he finished, Wieland claimed his finisher's medal and explained why he did it: "For the same reason as 20,000 other people. It's the greatest marathon in the country." He also cited three specific reasons: to show his born-again Christian faith; to test his conditioning; and to promote the President's Council on Physical Fitness, of which he is a member.

Wieland said, "Success is not based on where you start, it's where you finish, and I finished. The first step was the most difficult, after that, we were on our way home. The joy has been the journey."

—*THE DENVER POST*

DISCOVER*LIFE*

They Found Joy in a Book

Lesson 5

1. **What would you say to a person who asked, "How can I find joy in my life?"**

   Do you see Christianity as a joyful religion? Why or why not?

Transitional Comment

In this session we'll see people go from weeping to rejoicing, hearing God's Word, and celebrating God's goodness.

2. **Nehemiah 8:1-3**

[1]When the seventh month came and the Israelites had settled in their towns, all the people assembled as one man in the square before the Water Gate. They told Ezra the scribe to bring out the Book of the Law of Moses, which the LORD had commanded for Israel.

[2]So on the first day of the seventh month Ezra the priest brought the Law before the assembly, which was made up of men and women and all who were able to understand. [3]He read it aloud from daybreak till noon as he faced the square before the Water Gate in the presence of the men, women and others who could understand. And all the people listened attentively to the Book of the Law.

Introductory Comment

After the completion of the wall, Nehemiah begins registering the inhabitants of the city by families. Then the people of Judah assemble to begin a different kind of building project—spiritual rebuilding.

Questions

a. **Describe what happened on the first day of the seventh month.**

   Who requested the reading of the law?

   Who attended the reading?

   Whose authority was behind the law?

b. **How do the people respond?**

   What did their response to the reading of the law suggest about their attitude toward God? Their attitude toward the law?

Helpful Notes

- *seventh month.* September-October.
- *Water Gate.* A gate on the east side of Jerusalem, located near a spring of water.
- *Ezra the scribe and priest.* See Ezra 7:1-6 and 10:16.
- *Book of the Law of Moses.* Probably the first five books of the Bible, usually called the Pentateuch. The "Law of Moses" is much broader than a list of regulations. It sums up God's faithful relationship with the Israelites and tells the way they ought to live in order to reflect God's goodness and mercy in the world.

3. **Nehemiah 8:4-8**

[4]Ezra the scribe stood on a high wooden platform built for the occasion. Beside him on his right stood Mattithiah, Shema, Anaiah, Uriah, Hilkiah and Maaseiah; and on his left were Pedaiah, Mishael, Malkijah, Hashum, Hashbaddanah, Zechariah and Meshullam.

[5]Ezra opened the book. All the people could see him because he was standing above them; and as he opened it, the people all stood up. [6]Ezra praised the LORD, the great God; and all the people lifted their hands and responded, "Amen! Amen!" Then they bowed down and worshiped the LORD with their faces to the ground.

[7]The Levites—Jeshua, Bani, Sherebiah, Jamin, Akkub, Shabbethai, Hodiah, Maaseiah, Kelita, Azariah, Jozabad, Hanan and Pelaiah—instructed the people in the Law while the people were standing there. [8]They read from the Book of the Law of God, making it clear and giving the meaning so that the people could understand what was being read.

Questions

a. **How do the people show their readiness to hear the Word of God?**

   How did they respond to the Lord?

   What do you suppose they were thinking and feeling?

b. **What help do the Levites give?**

   Why was this important?

   What parallels this practice today?

Helpful Notes

- *the people all stood up.* It was customary in Jewish worship to stand for the Scripture reading—a sign of respect for God's Word.
- *lifted up their hands.* Expressed the people's desire to give their hearts to God.
- *Amen.* Means "so be it."
- *bowed down . . . with their faces to the ground.* A posture of humility and submission.
- *understand.* Have a thorough grasp, more than just knowing what was said.

4. **Nehemiah 8:9-12**

[9]Then Nehemiah the governor, Ezra the priest and scribe, and the Levites who were instructing the people said to them all, "This day is sacred to the LORD your God. Do not mourn or weep." For all the people had been weeping as they listened to the words of the Law.

[10]Nehemiah said, "Go and enjoy choice food and sweet drinks, and send some to those who have nothing prepared. This day is sacred to our Lord. Do not grieve, for the joy of the LORD is your strength."

11 The Levites calmed all the people, saying, "Be still, for this is a sacred day. Do not grieve."

12 Then all the people went away to eat and drink, to send portions of food and to celebrate with great joy, because they now understood the words that had been made known to them.

Questions

a. How do the people respond to the reading of the Law?

Why do you think they responded that way?

Why was it declared a day that was sacred to the Lord?

Why were they not to mourn or weep?

b. How are they to celebrate?

What reason did they have for joy?

Why is joy a better response than grief in this situation?

How were they to treat those who were in need?

What are ways in which faith in God brings joy today?

c. What was so significant about the people understanding the words of the Lord?

How important is understanding the words of the Lord today?

Helpful Notes

- *Nehemiah . . . Ezra . . . the Levites.* Note the unity of the civil leader (Nehemiah) and spiritual leaders.
- *sacred to the Lord.* Set apart for God's purposes.
- *weeping.* Showed the people's awareness that they had failed to keep God's Law. The focus of the day, however, was to be the celebration of how God delivered the people from both physical captivity and the captivity of sin.
- *send some to those who have nothing.* It was customary to remember the poor on festive occasions.

5. Nehemiah 8:13-18

13 On the second day of the month, the heads of all
the families, along with the priests and the Levites,
gathered around Ezra the scribe to give attention to
the words of the Law. 14 They found written in the Law,
which the LORD had commanded through Moses, that
the Israelites were to live in booths during the feast of
the seventh month 15 and that they should proclaim this
word and spread it throughout their towns and in
Jerusalem: "Go out into the hill country and bring back
branches from olive and wild olive trees, and from
myrtles, palms and shade trees, to make booths"—as it
is written.

16 So the people went out and brought back
branches and built themselves booths on their own
roofs, in their courtyards, in the courts of the house of
God and in the square by the Water Gate and the one
by the Gate of Ephraim. 17 The whole company that
had returned from exile built booths and lived in
them. From the days of Joshua son of Nun until that
day, the Israelites had not celebrated it like this. And
their joy was very great.

18 Day after day, from the first day to the last, Ezra read from the Book of the Law of God. They celebrated the feast for seven days, and on the eighth day, in accordance with the regulation, there was an assembly.

Questions

a. What command do the people find in the Law on the second day of the month?

Who was gathered around Ezra on this occasion?

b. What do they do about this discovery?

Describe how the feast of the seventh month was celebrated.

What was the end result of their festivities (v. 17)?

Why do you think this feast was particularly joyful?

c. What are the most important things we have discovered from Nehemiah so far?

How can we act on these discoveries?

Helpful Notes

- *written in the Law.* See Leviticus 23:33-43.
- *booths.* Temporary shelters made from tree branches. These recalled the days when the Israelites wandered in the desert after leaving Egypt.
- *feast of the seventh month.* Also called the Feast of Booths.
- *Gate of Ephraim.* On the north side of Jerusalem.
- *Joshua son of Nun.* Led the Israelites when they first entered Canaan and drove out their enemies.

Main Ideas

- At the people's request, the Law of God was read and explained.
- In response, the people first worshiped, then wept, and finally rejoiced.
- Responding obediently, they restored practices and laws that had been neglected.

Good News

Even if you have neglected God's Word, reading it again will bring the truth to light, will change lives, and will bring joy to your heart.

Optional Prayer Time

Ask group members to think about one or two things that bring them joy. Ask them to pray a simple prayer thanking God for those blessings. Tell them that as you pray around the circle, they can simply say, "Thank you, God, for the joy of ________."

Optional Accountability Question

Have you been robbing yourself of joy and power by not reading God's Word, like the people of Jerusalem before Nehemiah? What commitment will you make to be certain you read God's Word for even five minutes each day?

DISCOVER*LIFE*

They Found Joy in a Book

Lesson 5

Nehemiah 8:1-3

[1]When the seventh month came and the Israelites had settled in their towns, all the people assembled as one man in the square before the Water Gate. They told Ezra the scribe to bring out the Book of the Law of Moses, which the LORD had commanded for Israel.

[2]So on the first day of the seventh month Ezra the priest brought the Law before the assembly, which was made up of men and women and all who were able to understand. [3]He read it aloud from daybreak till noon as he faced the square before the Water Gate in the presence of the men, women and others who could understand. And all the people listened attentively to the Book of the Law.

Nehemiah 8:4-8

[4]Ezra the scribe stood on a high wooden platform built for the occasion. Beside him on his right stood Mattithiah, Shema, Anaiah, Uriah, Hilkiah and Maaseiah; and on his left were Pedaiah, Mishael, Malkijah, Hashum, Hashbaddanah, Zechariah and Meshullam.

[5]Ezra opened the book. All the people could see him because he was standing above them; and as he opened it, the people all stood up. [6]Ezra praised the LORD, the great God; and all the people lifted their hands and responded, "Amen! Amen!" Then they bowed down and worshiped the LORD with their faces to the ground.

[7]The Levites—Jeshua, Bani, Sherebiah, Jamin, Akkub, Shabbethai, Hodiah, Maaseiah, Kelita, Azariah, Jozabad, Hanan and Pelaiah—instructed the people in the Law while the people were standing there. [8]They read from the Book of the Law of God, making it clear and giving the meaning so that the people could understand what was being read.

Nehemiah 8:9-12

[9]Then Nehemiah the governor, Ezra the priest and scribe, and the Levites who were instructing the people said to them all, "This day is sacred to the LORD your God. Do not mourn or weep." For all the people had been weeping as they listened to the words of the Law.

[10]Nehemiah said, "Go and enjoy choice food and sweet drinks, and send some to those who have nothing prepared. This day is sacred to our Lord. Do not grieve, for the joy of the LORD is your strength."

[11]The Levites calmed all the people, saying, "Be still, for this is a sacred day. Do not grieve."

[12]Then all the people went away to eat and drink, to send portions of food and to celebrate with great joy, because they now understood the words that had been made known to them.

Nehemiah 8:13-18

[13]On the second day of the month, the heads of all the families, along with the priests and the Levites, gathered around Ezra the scribe to give attention to the words of the Law. [14]They found written in the Law, which the LORD had commanded through Moses, that the Israelites were to live in booths during the feast of the seventh month [15]and that they should proclaim this word and spread it throughout their towns and in Jerusalem: "Go out into the hill country and bring back branches from olive and wild olive trees, and from myrtles, palms and shade trees, to make booths"—as it is written.

[16]So the people went out and brought back branches and built themselves booths on their own roofs, in their courtyards, in the courts of the house of God and in the square by the Water Gate and the one by the Gate of Ephraim. [17]The whole company that had returned from exile built booths and lived in them. From the days of Joshua son of Nun until that day, the Israelites had not celebrated it like this. And their joy was very great.

[18]Day after day, from the first day to the last, Ezra read from the Book of the Law of God. They celebrated the feast for seven days, and on the eighth day, in accordance with the regulation, there was an assembly.

Questions

1. **What would you say to a person who asked, "How can I find joy in my life?"**
2. **Nehemiah 8:1-3**
   a. Describe what happened on the first day of the seventh month.
   b. How do the people respond?
3. **Nehemiah 8:4-8**
   a. How do the people show their readiness to hear the Word of God?
   b. What help do the Levites give?
4. **Nehemiah 8:9-12**
   a. How do the people respond to the reading of the Law?
   b. How are they to celebrate?
   c. What was so significant about the people understanding the words of the Lord?
5. **Nehemiah 8:13-18**
   a. What command do the people find in the Law on the second day of the month?
   b. What do they do about this discovery?
   c. What are the most important things we have discovered from Nehemiah so far?

STUDIES IN THIS SERIES

*after*Word

Good News at Work

I find joy in staying after men who need the Lord. I pick some tough targets. I pray for them, spend time with them, share my life with them, and then watch them come to Christ. Nothing pumps my tire like snatching someone from death to life.

I meet a man on his turf. I go to his business office or out to lunch wherever he wants to go. The thing that revs me up for preaching is the real-life working-out of the gospel as it changes the lives of men.

—BUFE KARRAKER IN *LEADERSHIP,* FALL 1998

Do You Know Yourself?

Most of us measure our sinfulness in one of two ways. We count our sins and for most of us, while realizing we are not perfect, we feel we score pretty well. Or we play the comparison game. The sense that we are not as bad as others bolsters our sense of being all right.

Unfortunately, our problem before a Holy God is not the amount of our sins, but the fact that we are sinners. Within us lies the potential for every heinous sin. When a public scandal is exposed, we express moral outrage—never considering that within each of us lies the potential for all of those sins and more. We could be the rapists, the child-abusers, the serial killers of our world. If it weren't for the inexplicable grace of God, they could have very well been us.

Before God, we are no different than the worst of these—we are just forgiven and by grace have been given new desires and opportunities to live for him.

If your relationship with God is about counting your sins, you will find it hard to adore your Savior. But if you realize that it is your sinfulness—not your sins—that nailed him to the tree, then you will never recover from the impact of that kind of mercy in your life. Until we recover an accurate view of ourselves in terms of the reality of our condition before God, we will not know how great his grace is, nor will our hearts acknowledge the debt we owe.

Affectionate adoration is the response of a heart that needs to be—and has been—forgiven much. It ignites from our recognition of the reality of our jeopardy before God and the inexhaustible grace and mercy he has shown us.

—JOSEPH M. STOWELL IN *MOODY,* JANUARY/FEBRUARY 2000

Gifts of Joy

God created two special gifts—laughter and music.

It's been shown that laughter has positive effects on the immune and cardiovascular systems. People who laugh readily get well quicker. So I seek laughter any way I can find it. Laughing at myself is one of the best things I do.

Music has the capacity to go straight through multiple emotional levels and sail right past my defenses. Music massages me at the deepest level. When I'm hurting, sometimes music is the only thing that reaches me, and it reaches me fast. I have no explanation for this except God has ordained it to be so.

Reconciliation brings me joy. I try not to get into situations where I have conflict or enemies, but everybody on the face of the earth does. There is a feeling that comes when you've made your enemy your friend that is unlike anything else.

Doing something creative brings joy to me. I'm sometimes mad at God that he's asked me to be a writer, because it's such hard work. But when I start with a blank sheet of paper and later see what I've written, that brings joy to me. It's the same as mowing my lawn or roto-tilling the garden. There's something about bringing order out of disorder, bringing something out of nothing, accomplishing something worthwhile or beautiful, that at the end of the day brings joy.

Successfully getting rid of things that sabotage my joy brings me joy. When I'm upset about something, and then I'm able to jettison that stuff out of my life, I feel good. I can take a breath of fresh air.

—RICHARD SWENSON IN *LEADERSHIP,* FALL 1998

A Puzzling Verse

Paul tells us in 1 Thessalonians 5:17 to "pray without ceasing." How can we accomplish this essential praying with so many other demands on our time?

Consider that when walking with a loved one, it is not necessary to communicate by talking all the time. I remember times walking with my wife, when for long periods we didn't exchange a word . . . yet the warmth of her hand in mine, her occasional glance, and the aura of her presence served as communication between us that exceeded any words.

That's the way we should walk with God, every minute of every day—aware of his continual presence, although not needing to talk to him every minute.

One way to pray to God throughout your day with him is by echoing the words God has spoken to us through Scriptures we have memorized.

I live in an area surrounded by hills and mountains. When I get the paper in the morning, I look at the gorgeous terrain and repeat Psalm 121, *"I lift up my eyes to the hills—where does my help come from? My help comes from the LORD, the Maker of heaven and earth."* What an inspiring way to start the day.

When troubling or inappropriate thoughts start crowding into my mind, I thank God for 2 Corinthians 10:4-5, *"The weapons we fight with are not the weapons of the world. . . . We demolish arguments . . . and we take captive every thought to make it obedient to Christ."*

A dozen times a day, verses of praise, comfort, support, and petition come to mind.

There is no substitute for the Scriptures. A thorough knowledge of the Bible offers us resources beyond our comprehension. If you want to experience the joy of praying without ceasing, memorize God's Word.

—WILLIAM R. NESBITT JR. IN *MOODY,* MARCH/APRIL 2000

DISCOVERLIFE

God Gives His People Joy

Lesson 6

1. **What value is there in making a promise?**

   Is it better to make a promise and risk not keeping it, or not to promise something but try to do it anyway?

2. **Nehemiah 9:1-3**

   1 On the twenty-fourth day of the same month, the Israelites gathered together, fasting and wearing sackcloth and having dust on their heads. 2 Those of Israelite descent had separated themselves from all foreigners. They stood in their places and confessed their sins and the wickedness of their fathers. 3 They stood where they were and read from the Book of the Law of the LORD their God for a quarter of the day, and spent another quarter in confession and in worshiping the LORD their God.

Introductory Comment

Twenty-four days after their first assembly and the reading of the Law, the people of Judah assemble again, this time to confess.

Questions

a. **Describe what happens at this assembly.**

   In what ways was it similar to the previous assembly (Neh. 8)? In what ways was it different?

   Why do you think they fasted and wore sackcloth?

   What did they do besides confess?

b. **Why do you think so much time is spent reading the Bible and confessing sin?**

   How easy is it for you to admit your guilt?

   How might your life be different if you consulted the Bible more often?

Helpful Notes

- *the same month.* September-October.
- *fasting.* Going without food for a period of time, especially as a way to dedicate oneself and one's time to God instead of to the usual routine of meals, etc.
- *wearing sackcloth and having dust on their heads.* Signs of mourning.
- *separated themselves from all foreigners.* Adopted a distinct lifestyle, including avoidance of intermarriage with immigrants who worshiped pagan gods.
- *the wickedness of their fathers.* The Israelites acknowledged not only their own wrongdoing before God but also the wrongs of their forefathers. They recognized here that they bore some responsibility not only for their individual sin but for the broken-down moral condition of their nation.

3. **Nehemiah 9:38**

   "In view of all this, we are making a binding agreement, putting it in writing, and our leaders, our Levites and our priests are affixing their seals to it."

   Nehemiah 10:28-33

   28 "The rest of the people—priests, Levites, gatekeepers, singers, temple servants and all who separated themselves from the neighboring peoples for the sake of the Law of God, together with their wives and all their sons and daughters who are able to understand—29 all these now join their brothers the nobles, and bind themselves with a curse and an oath to follow the Law of God given through Moses the servant of God and to obey carefully all the commands, regulations and decrees of the LORD our Lord.

   30 "We promise not to give our daughters in marriage to the peoples around us or take their daughters for our sons.

   31 "When the neighboring peoples bring merchandise or grain to sell on the Sabbath, we will not buy from them on the Sabbath or on any holy day. Every seventh year we will forgo working the land and will cancel all debts.

   32 "We assume the responsibility for carrying out the commands to give a third of a shekel each year for the service of the house of our God: 33 for the bread set out on the table; for the regular grain offerings and burnt offerings; for the offerings on the Sabbaths, New Moon festivals and appointed feasts; for the holy offerings; for sin offerings to make atonement for Israel; and for all the duties of the house of our God.

Introductory Comment

(Leaders may want to read aloud to the group the prayer of confession—or portions of it—from 9:5-37.) In the prayer recorded in Nehemiah 9:5-37, the Israelites recall how God dealt faithfully and fairly with them. They acknowledge him as their creator, as a gracious God who keeps all his promises and is even quick to forgive. They admit that they are an arrogant and disobedient people. Despite their sinful rebellion, God has not abandoned them but rather has punished them in love, as he had promised.

Now, having acknowledged their sin, they are ready to be restored to God's favor and to their position in the promised land. Following the confession, the people make a binding agreement with God.

Questions

a. **What binding agreement do the people make?**

   Who made this agreement?

   Why would they do this?

   To what extent would they obey God's law?

b. What do they promise regarding marriage? Regarding observance of the Sabbath? Regarding giving to the temple?

What was important about each of these?

Should we promise things to God? What might these promises include?

c. What impact would these commitments have upon Jewish social, economic, and religious life?

How should commitment to God affect a person's life today? How should it affect the lives of those around them?

Helpful Notes

- *curse and an oath.* Under oath the people invoked a curse on themselves in the event that they broke this pledge.
- *marriage to the people around us.* See Exodus 34:15-16 and Leviticus 20:26.
- *Sabbath.* The Jewish day of rest ordained by God, on which work ceased (see Ex. 20:8-11).
- *forgo working the land.* Old Testament law dictated that every seventh year was a year of rest in which the land was not to be cultivated (see Ex. 23:10-11; Lev. 25:4-7).
- *cancel all debts.* Old Testament law required the canceling of debts every seven years (see Deut. 15:1-3).
- *third of a shekel.* A shekel was a half-ounce silver coin.
- *bread set out on the table.* Twelve loaves set in two rows of six on a table in the temple. This symbolized God, as a host, inviting the people to have fellowship with him at a meal.

4. Nehemiah 10:35-37, 39

35"We also assume responsibility for bringing to the house of the LORD each year the firstfruits of our crops and of every fruit tree.

36"As it is also written in the Law, we will bring the firstborn of our sons and of our cattle, of our herds and of our flocks to the house of our God, to the priests ministering there.

37"Moreover, we will bring to the storerooms of the house of our God, to the priests, the first of our ground meal, of our [grain] offerings, of the fruit of all our trees and of our new wine and oil. And we will bring a tithe of our crops to the Levites, for it is the Levites who collect the tithes in all the towns where we work.

39"The people of Israel, including the Levites, are to bring their contributions of grain, new wine and oil to the storerooms where the articles for the sanctuary are kept and where the ministering priests, the gatekeepers and the singers stay. We will not neglect the house of our God."

Questions

a. What do the people promise to do?

What is significant about giving firstfruits and firstborn rather than later fruits and later born?

Do you put God first in the various areas of your life: work, family, friends, possessions, goals?

b. Where are these gifts brought?

Why should they be brought there?

Do you think God appreciates people giving to him today?

What do you think God expects?

Helpful Notes

- *house of the Lord.* The temple where God dwelt and the people came regularly to worship.
- *firstfruits.* First to be harvested (see Ex. 23:19).
- *firstborn.* Firstborn animals were usually the ones killed and offered as a sacrifice.
- *firstborn children.* These were redeemed, or "bought back," rather than slain as a sacrifice (see Num. 18:15-16).
- *tithe.* Ten percent.

5. Nehemiah 12:27-31, 38, 40, 43

27At the dedication of the wall of Jerusalem, the Levites were sought out from where they lived and were brought to Jerusalem to celebrate joyfully the dedication with songs of thanksgiving and with the music of cymbals, harps and lyres. 28The singers also were brought together from the region around Jerusalem—from the villages of the Netophathites, 29from Beth Gilgal, and from the area of Geba and Azmaveth, for the singers had built villages for themselves around Jerusalem. 30When the priests and Levites had purified themselves ceremonially, they purified the people, the gates and the wall.

31I had the leaders of Judah go up on top of the wall. I also assigned two large choirs to give thanks. One was to proceed on top of the wall to the right, toward the Dung Gate.

38The second choir proceeded in the opposite direction. I followed them on top of the wall, together with half the people—past the Tower of the Ovens to the Broad Wall. . . .

40The two choirs that gave thanks then took their places in the house of God; so did I, together with half the officials. . . .

43And on that day they offered great sacrifices, rejoicing because God had given them great joy. The women and children also rejoiced. The sound of rejoicing in Jerusalem could be heard far away.

Introductory Comment

With the work on the wall of Jerusalem completed and the enemies of Israel at bay, plans are made for a joyful dedication.

Questions

a. **What groups of people are brought in for this occasion?**

How were they to celebrate (v. 27b)?

What might the purification ritual have reminded the people of?

What was the mood of the people?

b. **What do the two choirs do?**

What was the purpose of these choirs?

c. **Why was giving thanks to God so appropriate at this moment?**

How had God been involved in this project?

Is giving thanks to God appropriate at this point in your life? Have you given him thanks?

Helpful Note

- *purified the people, the gates, and the wall.* The people shaved, cleansed their bodies, and washed their clothes. The wall was probably purified by ceremonial sprinkling of clean water. This act of purification was to teach God's holiness and remind Israel that God expected moral purity.

6. Nehemiah 12:44-45

44 At that time men were appointed to be in charge
of the storerooms for the contributions, firstfruits and
tithes. From the fields around the towns they were to
bring into the storerooms the portions required by
the Law for the priests and the Levites, for Judah was
pleased with the ministering priests and Levites.
45 They performed the service of their God and the
service of purification, as did also the singers and
gatekeepers, according to the commands of David
and his son Solomon.

Question

What was done to restore and sustain temple worship?

How were those who worked in the temple and led the worship supported financially?

How does worship today compare to worship in Nehemiah's day?

What motivates people to worship God?

Helpful Notes

- *service of purification.* Cleansing of all that was set apart for use in worship to God.
- *worship.* Originally "worth-ship." To worship is to experience and proclaim the worth of God.

Main Ideas

- Reading God's Word brought the people to confession of sin and to worship.
- Hearing the law, God's people responded by committing themselves to do what it required.
- The newly completed wall was joyfully dedicated, with thanks offered to its primary builder, the Lord.
- The renewed trust in God and focus on God's Word corresponded with a renewed desire to give God the worship and tithes he desired, which meant the reinstatement of temple worship.

Good News

Regardless of how they have lived in the past or whether they have fallen away from God, when people turn to God with sincere and humble hearts, God restores them to a close relationship and brings them joy.

Optional Prayer Time

As we can see from the example of the Israelites, one of the biggest motivations to worship is remembering what God has done. Have a time of prayer in which the group members can thank God for things he has done for them. Encourage them to make each thanksgiving brief, like "Thank you, God, for my children," but tell them that it's OK to speak up several times during the prayer. Then close the prayer time yourself.

Optional Accountability Question

Do you feel like worshiping God each week? Is anything lacking in your worship experience? What can you take from this study that might help your worship? How will you prepare to better worship God this week?

DISCOVER*LIFE*

God Gives His People Joy

Lesson 6

Nehemiah 9:1-3

[1]On the twenty-fourth day of the same month, the Israelites gathered together, fasting and wearing sackcloth and having dust on their heads. [2]Those of Israelite descent had separated themselves from all foreigners. They stood in their places and confessed their sins and the wickedness of their fathers. [3]They stood where they were and read from the Book of the Law of the LORD their God for a quarter of the day, and spent another quarter in confession and in worshiping the LORD their God.

Nehemiah 9:38

"In view of all this, we are making a binding agreement, putting it in writing, and our leaders, our Levites and our priests are affixing their seals to it."

Nehemiah 10:28-33

[28]"The rest of the people—priests, Levites, gatekeepers, singers, temple servants and all who separated themselves from the neighboring peoples for the sake of the Law of God, together with their wives and all their sons and daughters who are able to understand—[29]all these now join their brothers the nobles, and bind themselves with a curse and an oath to follow the Law of God given through Moses the servant of God and to obey carefully all the commands, regulations and decrees of the LORD our Lord.

[30]"We promise not to give our daughters in marriage to the peoples around us or take their daughters for our sons.

[31]"When the neighboring peoples bring merchandise or grain to sell on the Sabbath, we will not buy from them on the Sabbath or on any holy day. Every seventh year we will forgo working the land and will cancel all debts.

[32]"We assume the responsibility for carrying out the commands to give a third of a shekel each year for the service of the house of our God: [33]for the bread set out on the table; for the regular grain offerings and burnt offerings; for the offerings on the Sabbaths, New Moon festivals and appointed feasts; for the holy offerings; for sin offerings to make atonement for Israel; and for all the duties of the house of our God.

Nehemiah 10:35-37, 39

[35]"We also assume responsibility for bringing to the house of the LORD each year the firstfruits of our crops and of every fruit tree.

[36]"As it is also written in the Law, we will bring the firstborn of our sons and of our cattle, of our herds and of our flocks to the house of our God, to the priests ministering there.

[37]"Moreover, we will bring to the storerooms of the house of our God, to the priests, the first of our ground meal, of our [grain] offerings, of the fruit of all our trees and of our new wine and oil. And we will bring a tithe of our crops to the Levites, for it is the Levites who collect the tithes in all the towns where we work.

[39]"The people of Israel, including the Levites, are to bring their contributions of grain, new wine and oil to the storerooms where the articles for the sanctuary are kept and where the ministering priests, the gatekeepers and the singers stay. We will not neglect the house of our God."

Nehemiah 12:27-31, 38, 40, 43

[27]At the dedication of the wall of Jerusalem, the Levites were sought out from where they lived and were brought to Jerusalem to celebrate joyfully the dedication with songs of thanksgiving and with the music of cymbals, harps and lyres. [28]The singers also were brought together from the region around Jerusalem—from the villages of the Netophathites, [29]from Beth Gilgal, and from the area of Geba and Azmaveth, for the singers had built villages for themselves around Jerusalem. [30]When the priests and Levites had purified themselves ceremonially, they purified the people, the gates and the wall.

[31]I had the leaders of Judah go up on top of the wall. I also assigned two large choirs to give thanks. One was to proceed on top of the wall to the right, toward the Dung Gate.

[38]The second choir proceeded in the opposite direction. I followed them on top of the wall, together with half the people—past the Tower of the Ovens to the Broad Wall. . . .

[40]The two choirs that gave thanks then took their places in the house of God; so did I, together with half the officials. . . .

[43]And on that day they offered great sacrifices, rejoicing because God had given them great joy. The women and children also rejoiced. The sound of rejoicing in Jerusalem could be heard far away.

Nehemiah 12:44-45

[44]At that time men were appointed to be in charge of the storerooms for the contributions, firstfruits and tithes. From the fields around the towns they were to bring into the storerooms the portions required by the Law for the priests and the Levites, for Judah was pleased with the ministering priests and Levites. [45]They performed the service of their God and the service of purification, as did also the singers and gatekeepers, according to the commands of David and his son Solomon.

Questions

1. **What value is there in making a promise?**
2. **Nehemiah 9:1-3**
   a. Describe what happens at this assembly.
   b. Why do you think so much time is spent reading the Bible and confessing sin?
3. **Nehemiah 9:38; 10:28-33**
   a. What binding agreement do the people make?
   b. What do they promise regarding marriage? Regarding observance of the Sabbath? Regarding giving to the temple?

(continued on next page)

STUDIES IN THIS SERIES

Algonquin Park
A natural treasure, quintessential Canada

A land … of peace and tranquility … of lakes, forests, hills, valleys, … of teeming life — trees, wildflowers, moose, wolves, bears, bugs, frogs, turtles, fish, and birds. They all go about their lives oblivious to people.

Algonquin Park attracts visitors from around the world. They bask in the scenery, paddle, swim, and fish its waters, and watch its wildlife. Many wonder how it came to be. How does it work? What does the future hold? This book looks beneath the surface and into the past. It tells the story behind the scenery. It shows how bedrock, soil, plants, animals, and the atmosphere come together in an intricate dance that unites primal elements and living things into an eloquent beauty found nowhere else on earth.

We explore two central themes: the geological history of Algonquin Park, and its present-day ecology. We look briefly at its human history, the changes that people have made, and conclude by looking into a crystal ball to fathom the future.

A living museum

A visit to Algonquin Park can be like touring a living museum. There is much to see, much to enjoy, much to learn. This book is a guide to get you started.

This book is divided into sections that are like individual exhibits in a museum. Each exhibit, or major section, gives information that is complete in itself.

Technology: This small exhibit introduces you to the technology we use. Learn about imaging from air and space to show the big picture. Discover Geographic Information Systems (GIS) to take the Earth apart layer by layer, and then reassemble it for better understanding.

Geography: In the geography exhibit, you will see how Algonquin Park straddles a dome, and where it lies in relation to the Great Lakes and major cities and rivers. You will also learn how to zoom with pictures, maps, and your imagination: in for a close look, then out for a broad view, then in again to check on details. We conclude the geographic introduction with an overview from space that shows Algonquin Park in the context of its immediate surroundings.

Geology: This is a large exhibit that explores a vast sweep of geologic time, from 1500 million years ago to the present. Geologists have only recently deciphered some of the amazing things that have happened during that time. And there is a lot more for them to learn. But the story of Algonquin is much better understood than even 10 years ago. Experience the epic drama that created Algonquin, a saga of crashing continents, fiery lava flows, icy glaciers, and torrents of water.

Ecology: The climate, the shape of the land, the soils, the plants and the animals are interrelated in wonderful, subtle, and complex ways that are delightful to untangle and a joy to behold. The ecology exhibit explains basic ecology concepts and shows how they relate to the Algonquin environment.

Human history: You, as a visitor, are the latest in a long history of humans in this area. Learn how aboriginals, settlers, loggers, industrialists, artists, scientists, and campers have lived, worked, and played here over the centuries. Then consider the future of Algonquin for the next century and beyond.

See for yourself: Each of the main exhibits suggests locations where you can view interesting and significant examples of the topics discussed in that section. We also provide a list of trails and a companion satellite image-map of the Highway 60 corridor.

Contents

Technology to reveal the Earth

We are fleas on an elephant. In fact, in relation to the size of the Earth, we are 1000 times smaller than the fleas on an elephant. So it is no surprise that it has been difficult for humankind to map, explore, and understand our mother Earth. The twentieth century spawned tools that have helped immensely.

Aerial photography

"You can't see the forest for the trees." This ancient adage was finally overcome with the advent of aviation. In the early 1920s, cameras in airplanes were adopted as an effective way to map the land. In the 1922 Frank MacDougall cut his eye-teeth on an aerial forest survey of James Bay and brought his enthusiasm for air surveys to Algonquin Park in 1931. Current aerial mapping cameras make nine-inch square negatives and take several hundred 3-D stereo photos per roll. Maps of the park are updated periodically with the aid of photographs from the air.

Ontario Ministry of Natural Resources

Portion of an air photo of Algonquin Visitor Centre and surrounding area. Note the visibility of trees of various sizes.

The Earth as an onion

The Earth can be thought of as made up of many concentric layers, like an onion. In geophysics, these are often called "spheres". You already know the atmosphere. Other "spheres" of interest in our exploration of Algonquin Park include the biosphere (the layer of life), the hydrosphere (the layer of water), the pedosphere (the layer of soil) and the lithosphere (the layer of rocks).

This concept of layers helps us mentally take apart the earth, study each layer, and then re-assemble the layers to understand the integrated whole.

GIS

GIS stands for "Geographic Information System". In a GIS, a computer stores and displays geographic information in many layers — the "Earth as onion" concept. This powerful technology enables us to visualize and understand physical relationships that might otherwise be difficult to grasp. We can start with the "whole onion", peel away layers, and see what lies underneath. As you will see, these layers can be displayed in different ways to study what is going on.

Space imaging

Every day, satellites of many nations pass over the Earth, imaging its surface in different ways. During the last thirty years, imaging of the Earth from space has become commonplace both for weather forecasting and understanding the earth as an integrated whole.

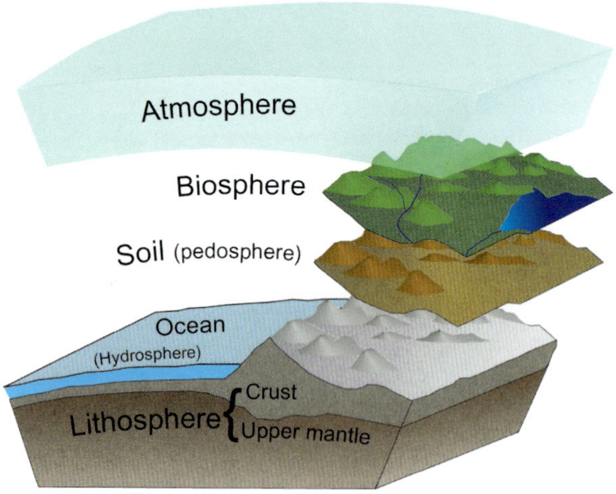

Geographic Information Systems allow us to examine the Earth layer by layer and put the pieces together for a complete picture.

Photo Courtesy NASA Goddard Space Flight Center

Artist rendition of the Landsat-7 satellite observing the Earth.

Satellites can make observations beyond the range our eyes can see. They produce digital images, ideal for study with GIS.

This book combines some of the most outstanding images of Algonquin Park with information from GIS technology. Now you too can share the insights previously restricted to specialists in the field.

Geographical context

The image below combines shading and colour to provide a vivid rendition of the topography of Algonquin Park and the surrounding area. The park itself lies near the Great Lakes region of North America, just north of Lake Ontario and northeast of Lake Huron. It lies on the highest part of a dome-shaped highland. Depending on where it lands, a raindrop falling on Algonquin Park can find its way westward to Lake Huron, northward to the Ottawa River, or east and south via one of several tributaries of the Ottawa River. The valley of the Ottawa River, north of the park, channels water from Lake Nippising and Lake Timiskiming (not shown) to the St. Lawrence River at Montreal. This valley was a major trade route for the aboriginal people of the area and for the earliest explorations of Europeans. It remains a major transportation artery today.

Two additional upland areas that are visible on this image are related geologically to Algonquin: the Laurentian Plateau north of the Ottawa Valley and the Adirondack Mountains of New York. These are parts of the Canadian Shield, made of ancient, hard rocks that make up the geologic core of North America.

The more densely populated areas of this region lie in the lowlands around the Great Lakes. Toronto, Montreal, Ottawa, North Bay, and Sudbury in Canada, and Buffalo, Rochester, Syracuse, and Albany in New York State all lie within a one-day drive.

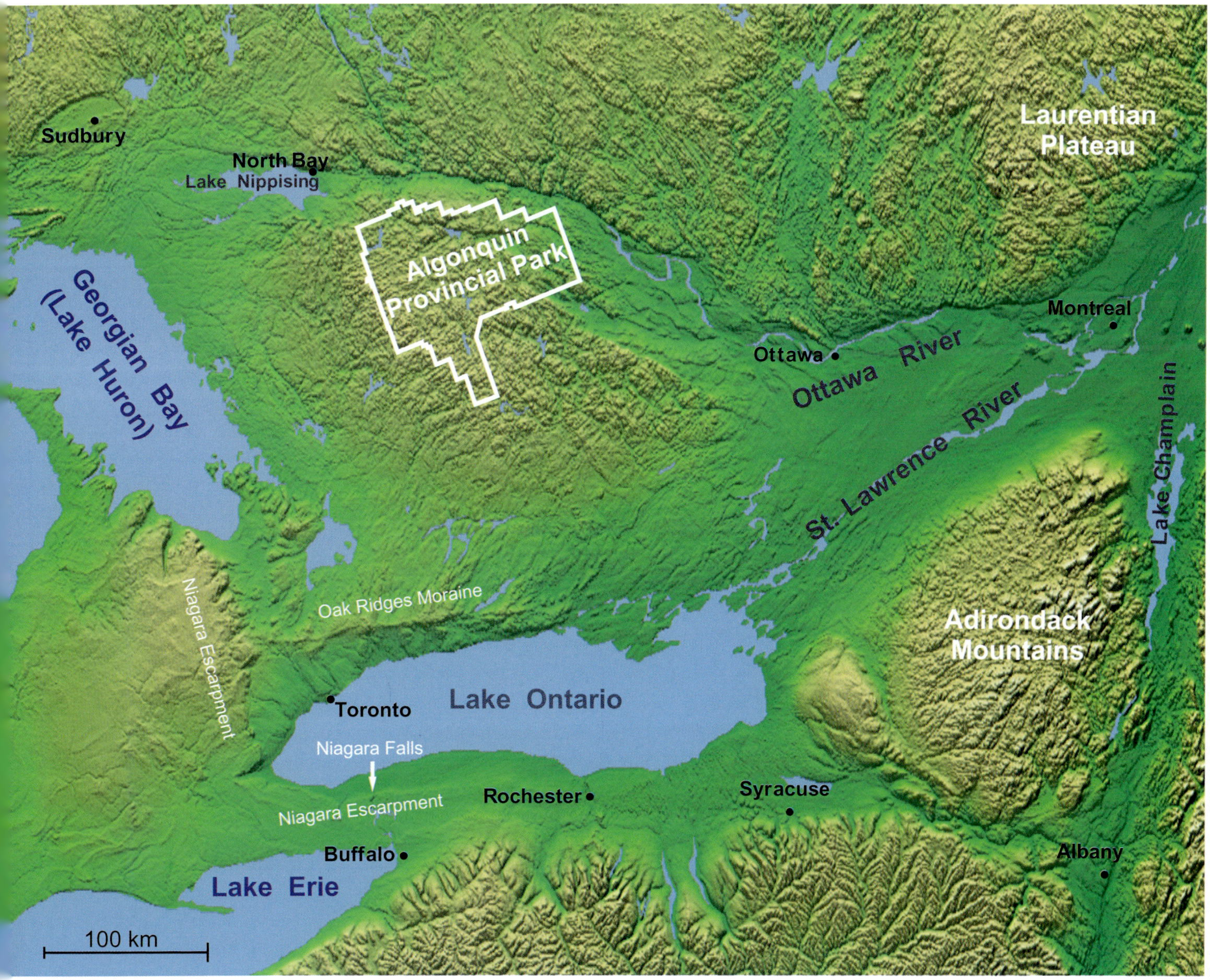

Background Image Courtesy NASA/Jet Propulsion Laboratory/Shuttle Radar Topographic Mapping Mission

Algonquin Park and its surroundings Algonquin Park straddles a highland area that lies north of Lake Ontario, north east of Lake Huron, and south of the Ottawa River valley. This image depicts topography using shading and colors that range from dark green for the lowest elevations to bright yellow and white at higher elevations.

Zoom-Zoom-Zoom!

Scale ~ 1:2000.
This is considered to be very "large scale".
It is used for engineering projects

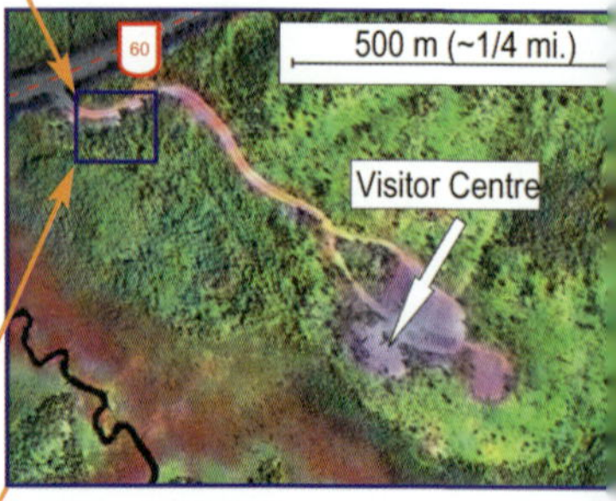

Scale ~ 1:20,000.
This scale is typical of aerial photography.
It is appropriate for detailed mapping forests.

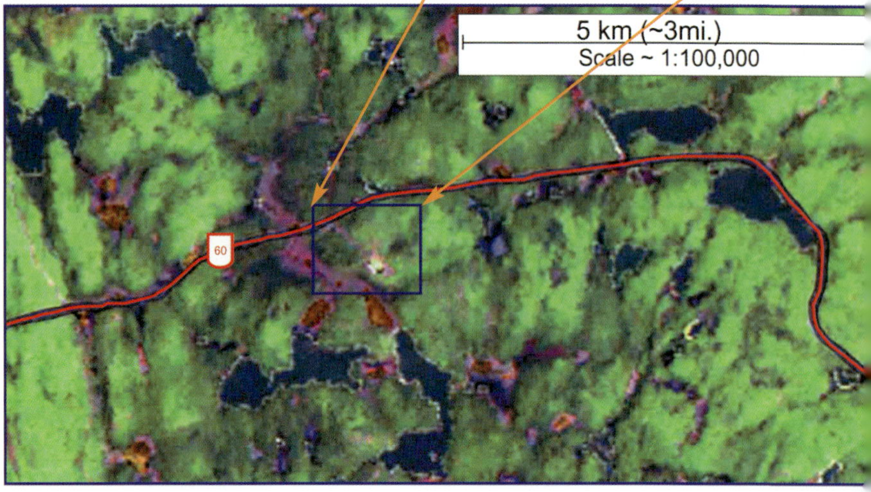

You can see the forest and the trees! With our ability to capture images and make maps at a wide range of scales, it is possible to study not just the trees and forest, but the hills, lakes, rivers and mountains. Exercise your imagination and learn to view Algonquin closely at first, and then from far away. Like looking through a zoom lens. This will help you understand how its various parts relate to each other and to their surroundings. The pictures on these two pages illustrate this concept and should help you get started.

We start with the twig of a common tree, a balsam fir. Backing off from our fir twig, we zoom out to an image at a scale of 1:2000. Now we can see the trees and their shadows along the road to the Visitor Centre. By going up in the sky, the trees no longer block our view of the forest. Next we zoom out ten times farther, to a scale of 1:20,000. Now we really can see the forest. In fact, foresters often use this scale for mapping forest stands. We can see a little piece of Highway 60 cutting across the top left corner, and when we zoom out to scales of 1:100,000 and then 1:500,000 we can see Highway 60 crossing through the southern part of Algonquin Park. Our final zoom takes us to a scale of 1:5 million, which enables us to see Algonquin Park in its regional context, as we discussed on the previous page.

The pictures on these pages show how information about plants, water bodies, and human constructions can be elicited at the different scales.

Overview from space

Now it is time to zoom in on Algonquin using the sharp eyes of the Landsat satellites (pages 8-9). Landsat observes the water and land surface cover (primarily vegetation in this image). We have used GIS technology to superimpose the roads, the Algonquin Park boundary (yellow line), and name some of the major water bodies, highways, and towns. Algonquin Park is surrounded by the highways, byways, and towns of Ontario. North Bay and Pembroke are the only cities, both small by global standards, with populations of 52,000 and 15,000 in 2001. All of the other towns on this image have populations of less than 10,000. Highway 17, a section of the Trans-Canada highway, follows the ancient route of Indians and voyageurs along the Ottawa River north of Algonquin. Highway 11, the principal north-south route between Toronto and northern Ontario, lies west of Algonquin. It is a major route of commerce and carries huge numbers of cottagers and tourists up from the south and back home again every weekend in the spring, summer, and fall.

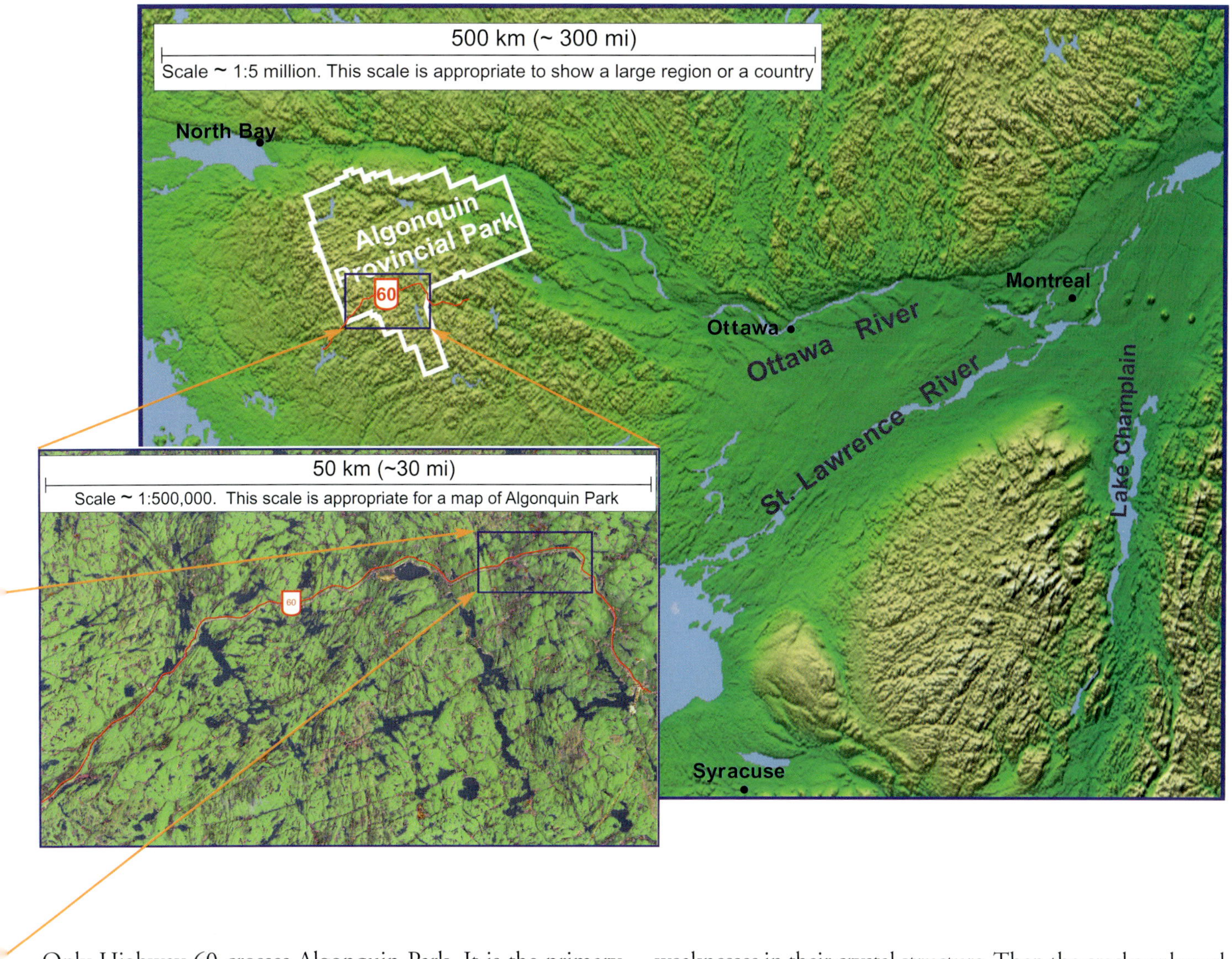

Only Highway 60 crosses Algonquin Park. It is the primary access route for visitors. All other roads penetrate from the edges, so the only reason to use them is for business specifically related to the park. This arrangement of roads, and their absence in the interior, preserves the natural character of Algonquin's interior.

This satellite image shows the many lakes of Algonquin and its surroundings. Different types of vegetation stand out. Broadleaf forests of maple, oak, poplar, and birch are bright green, while conifer stands of pine, spruce, fir, hemlock and larch appear dark green. Note that the "hardwood hills" of the western part of the park are bright green, and there is much more dark green in the lowlands to the east. The valleys throughout the park contain conifers because these trees tend to grow in sites with low soil fertility, which is characteristic of valleys (see page 28 and the following pages). In the northwest corner we can see some long straight valleys that appear to follow geological fault lines. In one place, several valleys intersect at a 45-degree angle. This is a case where the tiny crystal structure of the rocks is magnified a million times or more to be visible from space! First the rocks cracked along weaknesses in their crystal structure. Then the cracks enlarged as water seeped in and erosion proceeded. Then the glaciers came along and gouged out the debris in the cracks, forming steep, narrow valleys. Then a forest of conifers populated the valleys, making them visible from space.

Purplish areas are forests with thin crowns. This can be the result of logging, or of damage such as that caused by insect infestations, windstorms, or ice storms. Wetlands can range from purple to pink to brown or yellow, depending on the type of vegetation that the satellite sees.

Outside Algonquin Park, the vegetation looks similar. It is apparent that Algonquin is not an island of green surrounded by farming, logging, mining, or urban sprawl. There is some agriculture near the Ottawa River, but far less than 100 years ago. Small examples of logging can be found here and there; mining is limited to numerous very small gravel pits scattered across the landscape. All in all the visible impact of humanity on the land surface remains mild in this part of Ontario. Other than the towns and small cities, the largest visible imprint is the military training area associated with the Canadian Forces Base at Petawawa.

North Bay
Mattawa
533
17
Lake Nipissing
654
11
534
522
124
520
518
Kioshkowi Lake
Manitou Lake
Cedar Lake
Hogan Lake
Lake Lavieille
Valleys following faults intersecting at 45 degrees.
Lake Opeonga
Canoe Lake
Smoke Lake
Lake of Two Rivers
60
Huntsville
Skeleton Lake
141
Kawagama Lake
Lake of Bays
ake Muskoka
Bracebridge

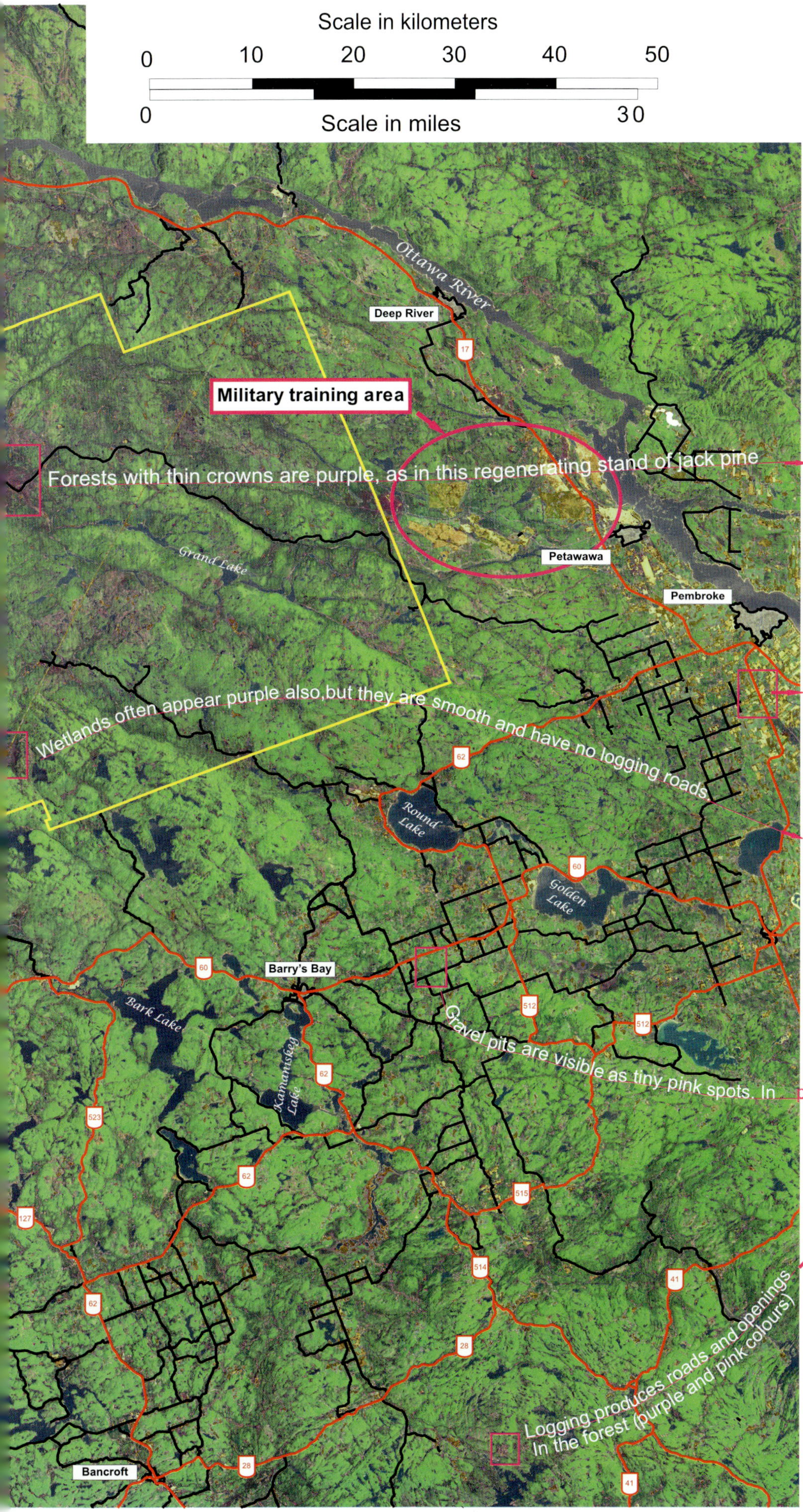

Algonquin Provincial Park and Surrounding Area

This map shows the water and vegetation of Algonquin Park and its surroundings. Broadleaf forests are bright green, while conifer forests are darker green. Features of particular interest are described below, enlarged as needed to show the necessary detail.

Farmland exhibits a typical patchwork of coloured rectangles and other shapes.

populated areas

Line colors

Yellow: Algonquin Park boundary
Red: Major highways
Black: Secondary roads

Landsat images acquired during summer seasons between 1995 and 2000 courtesy Canada Centre for Remote Sensing.

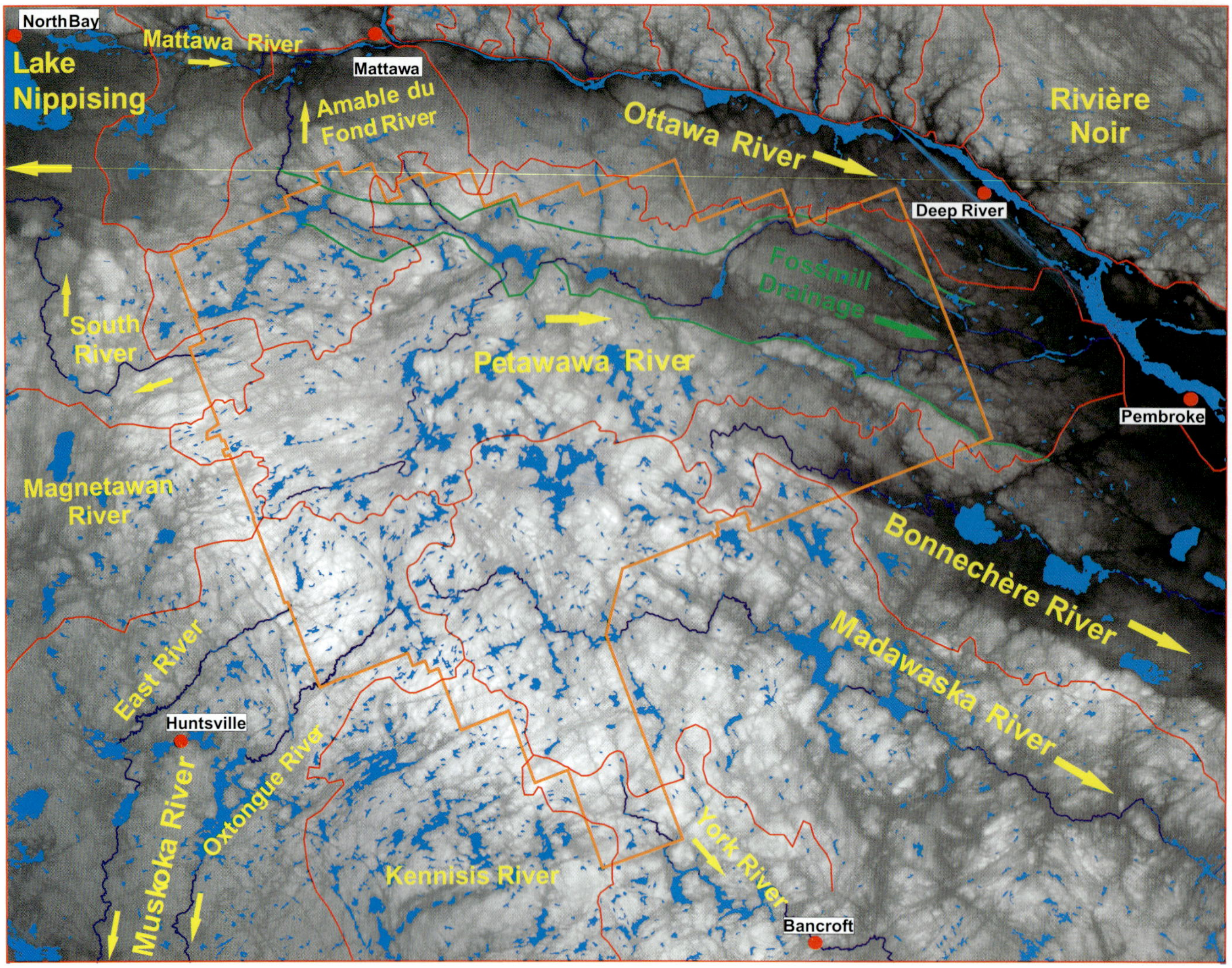

Topographic data made available through the US Geological Survey Earth Resources Observation Satellite Data Center from data provided by the NASA/JPL Shuttle Radar Topographic Mapping Mission.

The lay of the land

The shape – or lay – of the land determines how water flows. When rain falls or snow melts, the unrelenting power of gravity forces water to find the most efficient path to the lowest point, the sea. Streams flow downhill. Lakes form when a bowl-like depression in the land interrupts flowing water. The bowl fills, and the stream flows on. Streams converge to make rivers, and rivers flow to the sea.

This aspect of the natural world has shaped culture, conflict, and trade throughout history. Aboriginal peoples defined and defended their territories on the basis of drainage basins; indeed, Algonquin is the name of the people whose territory is defined by the water that flows into the Ottawa River.

Putting GIS to work, the map above shows the topography as shades of gray: brighter is higher and darker is lower. The shape of the land is now apparent: Algonquin Park (orange boundary line) straddles a dome. It is the source of many rivers, which flow outward in all directions. The park was created mainly to prevent clearing the land, which would cause flooding in the spring, drought in the summer, and poor water quality year round.

The red lines outline the drainage basins of the rivers flowing out of Algonquin Park. The Petawawa, the Bonnechère, and the Madawaska are all tributaries of the Ottawa, and flow southeast, following major fault lines. Three branches of the Muskoka River, (the East, the Oxtongue, and the Kennisis rivers), flow west toward Lake Huron. The York River flows to the south and eventually joins the Madawaska. But water does not leave the Algonquin dome easily. Instead many depressions in the land form thousands of lakes, making Algonquin Park a canoeing paradise.

Outside Algonquin we find lower areas: Lake Nippising to the northwest and the broad Ottawa Valley to the east. These are connected by a narrow groove in the Earth. Here flow the Mattawa and upper Ottawa rivers, merging at the town of Mattawa.

Algonquin's dome and the many lake-forming depressions present a wonderful area. Why do we have a dome? Why so many lakes? How they came to be is explained by looking at the geological history of the area. The first part is amazingly old; the second is remarkably recent. Both are fascinating.

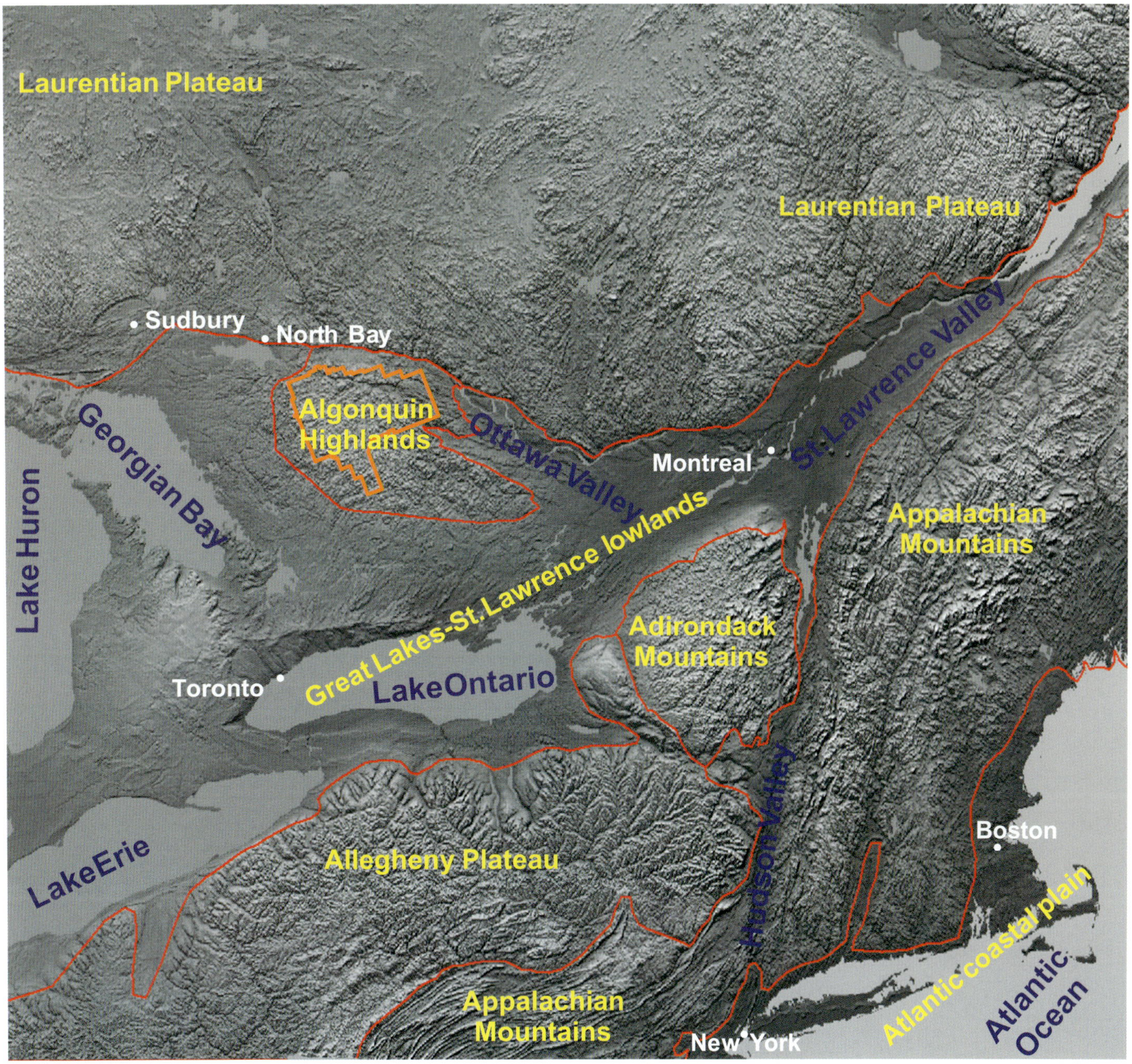

Topographic image courtesy NASA/JPL Shuttle Radar Topographic Mapping Mission.

The uplands and lowlands around Algonquin

The formation of the land of Algonquin Park is an amazing saga. It is the story continents crashing together, mountains rising and wearing away, oceans forming and disappearing. And, of course, ice ages. To set the stage for this tale we must back off and take in a wider view.

Our geological journey begins with a broad overview that spans the northeast from New York City into northern Ontario and Québec. The background image shows the topography. The red lines delineate areas similar to each other called physiographic regions. The Laurentian Plateau stretches across the top of the image. This is a vast area of rolling terrain covered with trees and lakes. It forms part of the Canadian Shield, the oldest area in North America. The Algonquin Highlands look like a southward extension of the Laurentian Plateau, and they are. Farther south, a broad lowland extends across the image. This is where we find the Great Lakes and the St. Lawrence Valley, with the Ottawa Valley jutting off to the northwest. Crossing this lowland into the United States, we find more uplands. The Adirondack Mountains and the Appalachian Mountains are the highest in the east. The Allegheny Plateau is a bucolic area of rolling hills that sport a mosaic of farms and forests. Approaching the Atlantic Ocean, we reach the densely-populated coastal plain that hosts the economic powerhouse of the American northeast. But North America does not stop at the shore; rather it extends hundreds of kilometres out to the edge of the continental shelf.

The formation of Algonquin is tied up in the formation of this entire area, so we must delve into it.

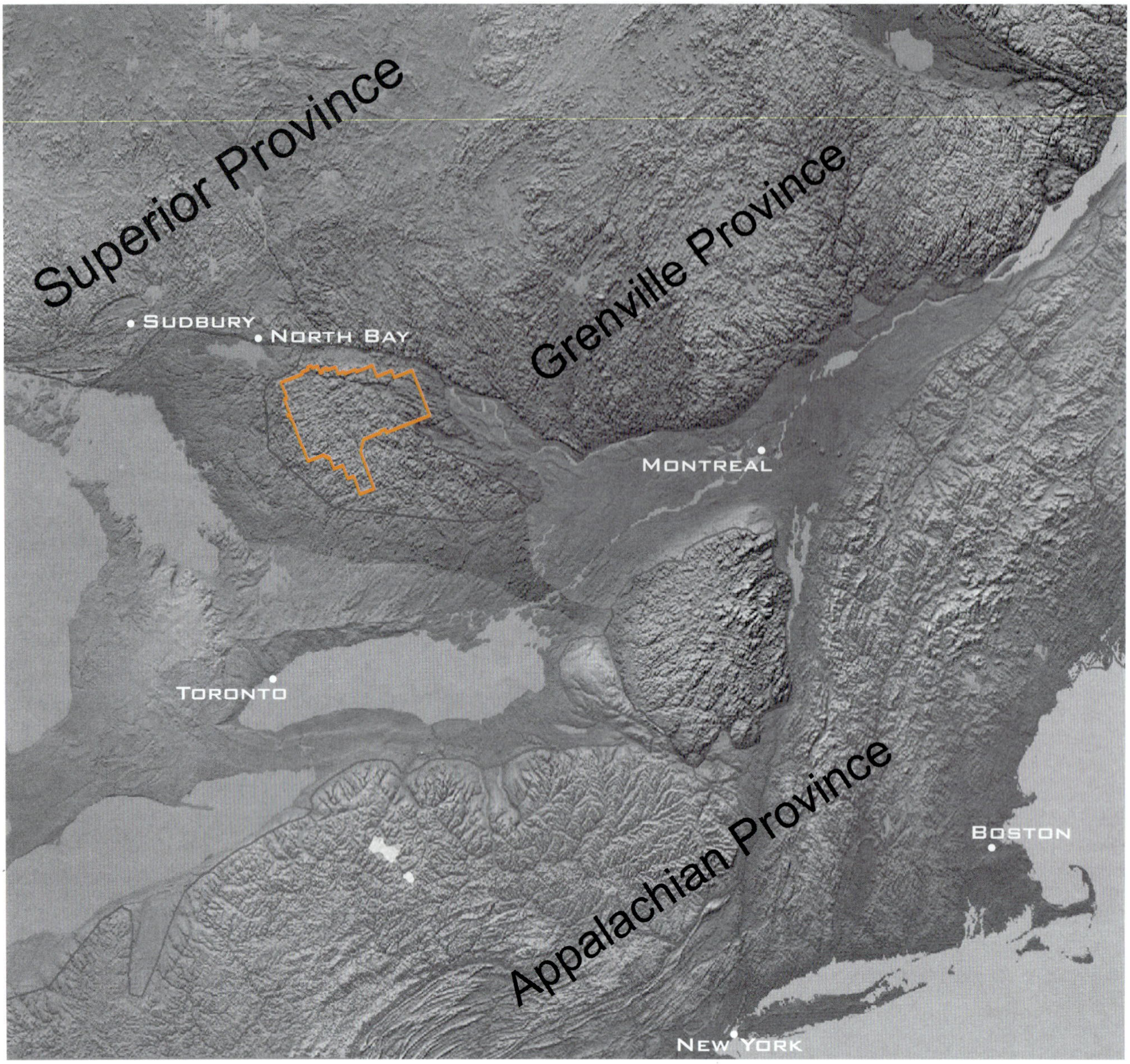

Topographic image courtesy NASA/JPL Shuttle Radar Topographic Mapping Mission.

Puzzle pieces

One of the greatest earth-shattering accomplishments in science has been unravelling continental drift. This led to a much greater understanding of mountains, volcanoes, earthquakes, and the Earth's geologic history. We now know that the continents are the thicker parts of plates that float on softer rock below and slowly move around the surface of the earth, like immense ice floes. As geologists around the world puzzled over their data, they have concluded that the continents themselves were assembled from smaller pieces. We will explain how this happens on page 13, and describe the formation of Algonquin Park on pages 14 and 15. Here we are just looking at three pieces of North America as we find them today.

The map above shows the pieces. They have been named "provinces" by geologists. The Superior Province (yellow) formed the margin of ancestral North America when we pick up the story of Algonquin's formation about 1500 million years ago. The Grenville Province (purple) is a huge swath of continental crust that was added along the edge of the Superior Province. Algonquin Park is found within the Grenville Province. Much of the Grenville Province is currently buried under the Appalachian Province (light blue), another huge swath of continental crust that was added later. The Adirondack Mountains in New York are part of the Grenville Province. The narrow purple neck that crosses the St. Lawrence River just downstream of Lake Ontario is an exposure of Grenville rocks that connects the Adirondacks to Algonquin. This is the Frontenac Arch, a bulge in the Grenville rocks that was once covered by sedimentary rocks of the Appalachian Province. Those softer sedimentary rocks have been eroded away over the bulge.

Layer upon layer

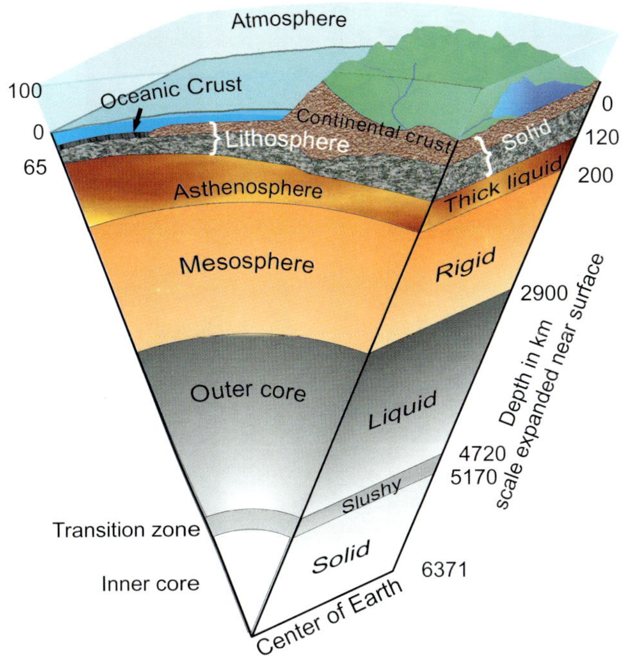

Our onion-Earth is organized into layers by gravity. During the time since the Earth formed, gravity has pulled the densest materials to the centre causing the lighter materials to "float" to the top. So now we have a core of iron and an atmosphere of gasses. The diagram at right shows the layering as it exists today. The only layers we need to be concerned with here are the lithosphere (a solid rock layer) and the asthenosphere.

The asthenosphere consists of molten rock that can flow slowly, somewhat like molasses in January. The lithosphere literally floats on the asthenosphere. The uppermost part of the lithosphere is called the crust. There are two types of crust, oceanic crust and continental crust. Oceanic crust is dense but thin: only about 5 km thick. It makes up the floor of the deep ocean. Continental crust is less dense but thicker. It makes up our land areas plus the continental shelves. Continental crust can rise as much as 9 km above sea level in the Himalayas. Like an iceberg, there is much more below the surface: continental crust can extend down to 40 or 50 km below sea level. Because is floating like an iceberg or a ship, continental crust plunges the deepest where there are high mountains to support, and not so far under lowlands.

Plates in motion

The lithosphere is broken into curved plates likes the surface of an egg with cracks in its shell. These plates are slowly moving around the surface of the Earth. Where two plates are pulling apart, new crust comes up as lava from the lithosphere and asthenosphere to fill the gap.

Where two plates are pushing together, one rides on top of the other. The edge of the lower plate is forced down into the Earth, a process called subduction. This is a violent process that releases a lot of energy in the form of earthquakes and volcanoes.

In the ocean, volcanoes form and create a chain of volcanic islands that can eventually merge into a large island arc like Japan, as shown below. When the lower lithosphere plunges under a continent, this typically forms a range of mountains, with some volcanoes, like the Andes.

The most dramatic event occurs when two pieces of continental crust collide with each other. The two pieces of crust are shoved together and the weaker crust breaks and gets thrust up into high mountains. This is happening today. India is crashing into southern Asia, pushing the continental crust into the huge pile we call the Himalayas.

All of these processes, and more, have taken place during the long geologic history of Algonquin Park.

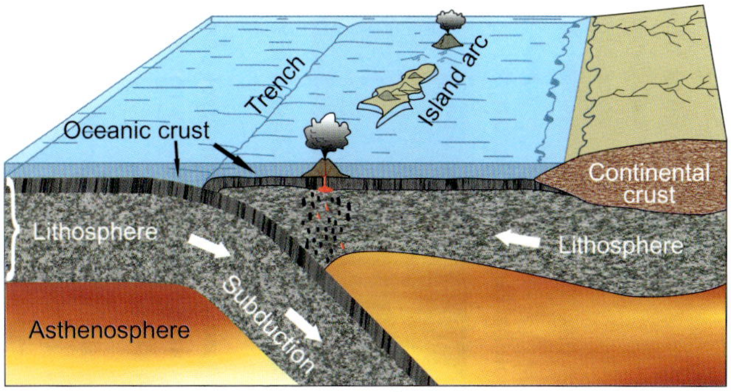

An island arc is formed when subduction occurs in an ocean.

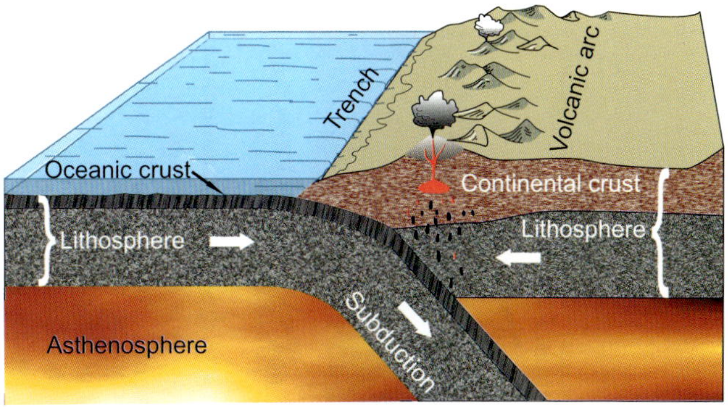

A mountain chain is formed when subduction occurs under the edge of a continent.

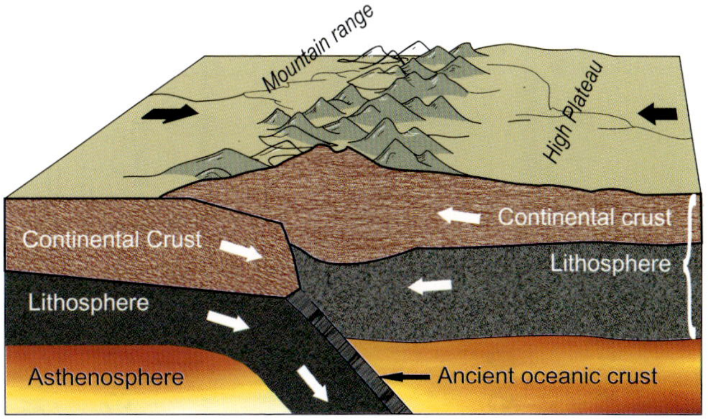

Lofty mountains are formed when two continents collide.

Graphics on this page are adapted from "This Dynamic Earth" by W. Jacquelyne Kios and Robert I. Tilling, courtesy US Geological Survey

See for yourself

In many places along Highway 60 rock cuts slice into bedrock like a knife cutting into a layered cake. These cuts provide a glimpse into the past.

Geologists classify rocks into three groups according to their origin.

Sedimentary rocks are formed from layers of sediments deposited under water. Rock beds can accumulate many kilometres thick over millions of years.

Igneous rocks solidify directly from molten magma.

Metamorphic rocks have changed their mineral structure as a result of heat or pressure or both. The heat and pressure can come from magma welling up from below, from being buried under thick piles of rocks when crustal plates collide, and other processes.

Along Highway 60 many of the rocks you see exposed in the cuts began their lives as igneous rocks deep inside the mountains formed near the coast of Nena, about 1450 million years ago. Some metamorphism happened at that time. Over the following 300 million years or so the mountains eroded away. When parts of Atlantica crunched into Nena between about 1200 to 1000 million years ago, it rode up over Nena. This caused extensive shearing that produced the layering visible in the rock cuts. Magma forced its way into cracks and slowly cooled into veins of granite and similar rocks. The landscape we now see was depressed to depths of 25 to 30 kilometres, where more metamorphism occured. The overlying rocks subsequently eroded away over hundreds of millions of years.

These massive layers of gneiss show the tilting that helps produce today's hills and valleys.

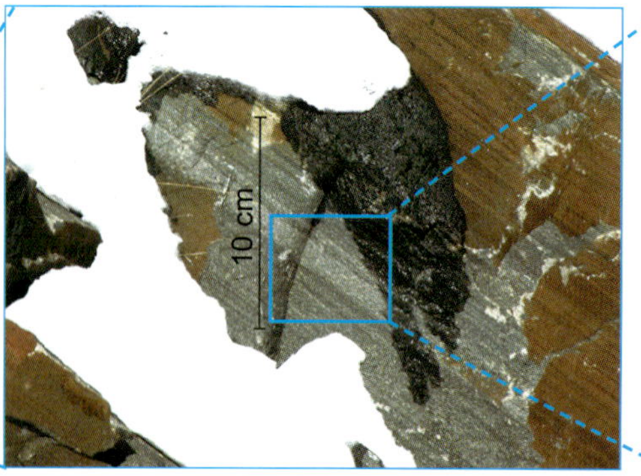

Most of the exterior is weathered to a rust-orange colour. In winter, pieces frequently break off, exposing the rock's true colours.

Looking closer, we see the light and dark gray bands and crystal structure characteristic of gneiss.

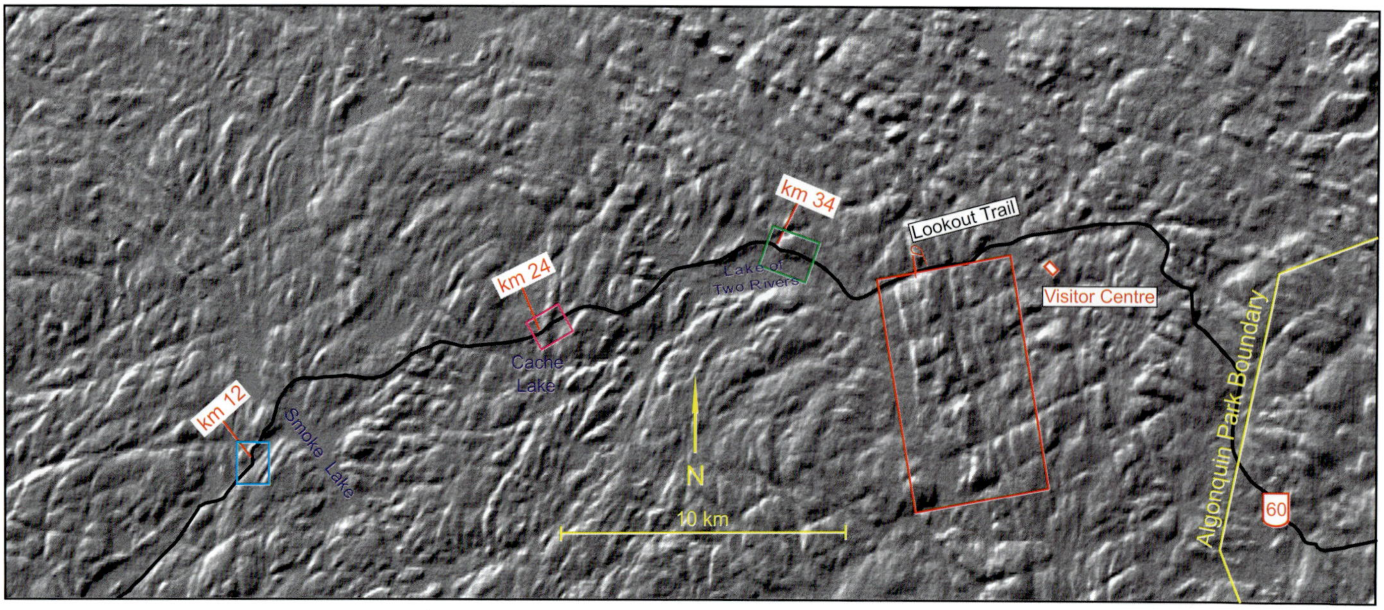

Topographic data courtesy NASA/JPL Shuttle Radar Topographic Mapping Mission

This is a shaded-relief map of Algonquin's topography near the Highway 60 corridor (black line). The hills and ridges are formed from layers of more resistant rock, while the valleys form where rock is more readily eroded. This complex topography suggests the tortured history of the underlying rocks. Each photo is framed with a colour. The coloured boxes in the map above show where the photo was taken.

These hills can be seen looking south from post 7 of the Lookout Trail (see red arrow in map on previous page). We see hills with steeper slopes to the right (west). Geologists infer tilted layers of rock that we have emphasized with red lines. The weaker layers erode more quickly, forming valleys, while the more resistant layers form ridges and hills.

A close-up look at the intruded feldspar-rich granite, the large mass with coarse pink crystals near the middle of the photo.

Granite has forced its way into cracks in the gneiss. The heat from this event has caused partial melting of the nearby rock, resulting in a mixture of gray and pink bands.

Evidence of a long and tortured history. The original igneous rocks have become layered gneiss through heat, pressure, and shearing forces. Feldspar-rich magma was injected into cracks, forming veins that cut across the layers and were subsequently deformed (wiggly white vein). These events took place over a span of 400 million years or more.

Algonquin under ice

While geologic events spanning 1500 million years created the overall shape of the land, Algonquin Park benefits greatly from many features bequeathed by the ice age.

What are ice ages, anyway, and why do they happen?

At times, like now, snow and ice have covered the poles. During these times, ice has frequently descended half-way or more to the equator: an ice age. However, throughout most of its history, Earth has been ice-free, even to the poles. What causes the temperature of the poles to fluctuate between frigid and balmy?

The sun is our reliable and consistent furnace. The atmosphere and oceans retain the sun's heat and circulate it from the equator to the poles. Most of the time (geologic time, that is), enough heat makes it to the poles to keep them ice-free. Sometimes, however, continents move into positions that impede this circulation, and the polar regions cool off. The current theory blames our present cold poles on South America and India, which have moved into positions that block previous circulation patterns that kept the poles warm. Once the circulation falters, ice ages become possible. Small changes in the Earth's orbit then determine whether there is enough heating in summer to melt last winter's snow. When it is cool enough that some snow persists through the summer, glaciers begin to form. Snow and ice reflect sunlight, increase the cooling, and a new ice age begins.

Algonquin Park iced over about 115,000 years ago and melted only about 11,000 years ago. That is a long time to be buried under a thick, heavy, cold, nearly-lifeless layer of frozen water. This ice totally disrupted the drainage. Before the glaciers arrived, a landscape of hills, valleys, and rivers carried water back to the oceans. A few small lakes may have nestled here and there; far fewer than there are now. But we can thank the glaciers for the many lakes we enjoy today. First, they scooped the soil from depressions in the bedrock, providing places for water to accumulate. Then they dropped sand, gravel, and rock haphazardly, impeding creeks and streams.

The moving glacier

While an ice age is in full-swing, glaciers are always on the move. Storms deposit more snow in some areas than others, resulting in thicker accumulation. The greater weight causes the ice to flow. It behaves somewhat like Silly-Putty, oozing along like a thick liquid unless it is stressed too much, in which case it cracks and breaks. While flowing, the ice scrapes the ground under it. As it accumulates debris, the glacier acts like sandpaper, becoming even more effective at scouring the surface underneath. After thousands of years of such pummelling, it is not surprising that scratches mar the gneiss and granite of Algonquin's bedrock.

Thomas V. Lowell

This is what the land looks like when it is covered with a continental ice sheet. Snow accumulates in the uplands, then compresses into ice that slowly oozes downhill.

In addition to gouging soil out of depressions so lakes can form, the glaciers have also widened, deepened and steepened valleys in Algonquin Park. The most notable example is the Barron Canyon, which sports a spectacular 100 metre vertical cliff face.

Glaciers can move huge boulders for long distances. These are called "erratics" because they do not match the rock types of the surrounding area. You can see one example of a glacial erratic at Post 2 on the Lookout Trail.

The melting glacier

Melting glaciers formed small but important features after the slow-moving ice sheets started to recede. **Glacial till,** the material the glacier was carrying, is the most widespread. (See map on page 22.) Glacial till consists of minerals in all sizes: silt, clay, sand, pebbles, and boulders. In Algonquin, the layer of till usually lies less than one metre deep over the bedrock.

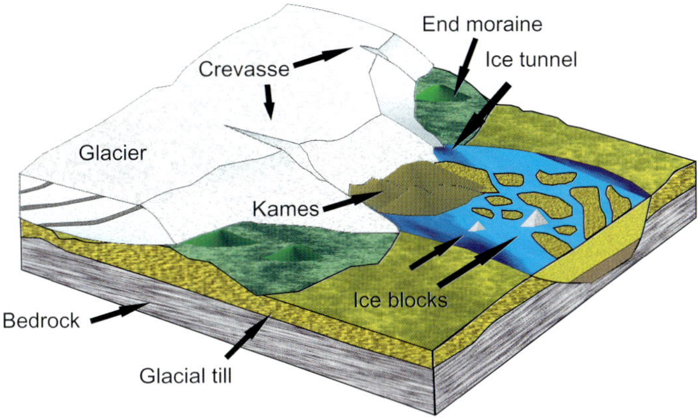

The ice in the glacier continues to move away from its centre of accumulation even as the edge melts. So the moving ice acts like a conveyor, bringing debris to the melting edge and dropping it there. Two things can happen then. If the melting water is flowing away in streams, the material from the glacier will form **outwash deposits**. In this case, the heavier material, rocks and gravel, will be dropped almost immediately, the sand will be carried further before it settles, and the silt will be carried along until the water enters a lake or the sea and stops flowing. So glacial outwash deposits become sorted, with the coarsest material nearest the source, and finer material further away. As the glacier retreats, finer material can be deposited on top of coarser material that was deposited earlier. The map on page 22 shows a large area covered by glacial outwash deposits in the northeast corner of Algonquin Park where the Fossmill drainage widens. This channel carried immense volumes of meltwater for a few centuries. When the channel widened, the water slowed down, depositing a thick "outwash plain" of sand inside the park and in the military training area near Petawawa.

If hills or ice restrict the water, the material will be deposited near the edge of the ice. Then it is called an **ice contact deposit**. Moving water does not sort the material, so ice contact deposits are essentially piles of sand and gravel. **Kames** and **end moraines** are two common forms of ice contact deposits.

When the glacier is melting, rivers flow in tunnels under the ice. **Eskers**, long and winding ridges, are the lasting imprint of the long-gone ice tunnels.

Sometimes while the glacier melts, a large block of ice will break off and become surrounded and possibly covered by debris. When this block finally melts, it leaves a lasting imprint as a kettle-shaped depression, which may contain a **kettle lake** thousands of years later.

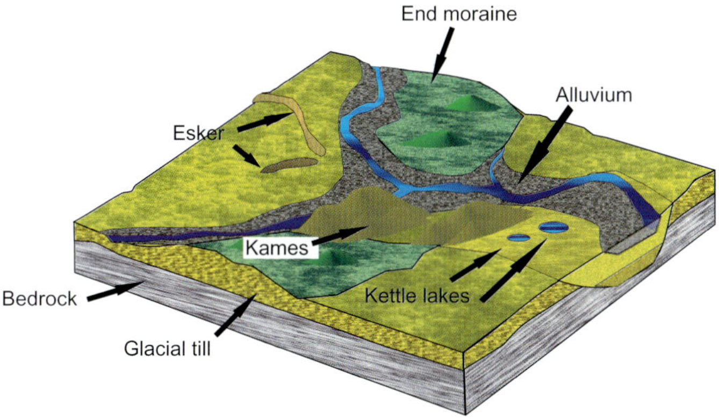

An illustration of some glacial features that are formed as a glacier is melting (left), and what the same area looks like in the future after the glacier is gone (right).

Illustration adapted from "Guide to the geology along Interstate 75 between Toledo and Cincinnati", courtesy of Ohio Department of Natural Resources, Ohio Geological Survey.

When the glacial water empties into a lake, it will leave sand (**coarse lacustrine deposits)** near its point of entry, while silt and clay (**fine lacustrine deposits)** can settle throughout the lake. Most of the fine lacustrine deposits can be found along the populated Highway 11 corridor, west of Algonquin. (See map on page 22.) This is no coincidence. They make the best farmland, so this area was settled earlier and more densely than areas with poorer soil.

Common surface deposits formed by glacial action

Till	Undifferentiated mixture of rocks, sand, and silt.
Ice contact deposits	Sand and gravel formed in the shapes of eskers, kames, and moraines, deposited under the ice or very near the ice edge.
Outwash deposits	Fans and deltas of sand and gravel deposited by meltwater away from the ice edge.
Fine lacustrine deposits	Silt and clay deposited in lakes.
Coarse lacustrine deposits	Sand and gravel deposited along beaches and near shore in lakes.
Marine deposits	Sand, silt and clay deposited in salt water (the Champlain Sea).
Alluvium	Gravel, sand, silt, and clay deposited on modern flood plains.

The End of the Ice Age

Ice ages end abruptly. The following four pictures illustrate the rapid retreat of the North American ice sheet in the area around Algonquin Park.

13,000 years ago the continental ice sheet was retreating northwards. Ice still covered Ontario, New York, and New England. Of the Great Lakes, only the Lake Erie area was ice-free. It contained a larger lake called Lake Iroquois. Ice prevented today's outflow to the St. Lawrence River, and Lake Iroquois drained into the Mississippi River.

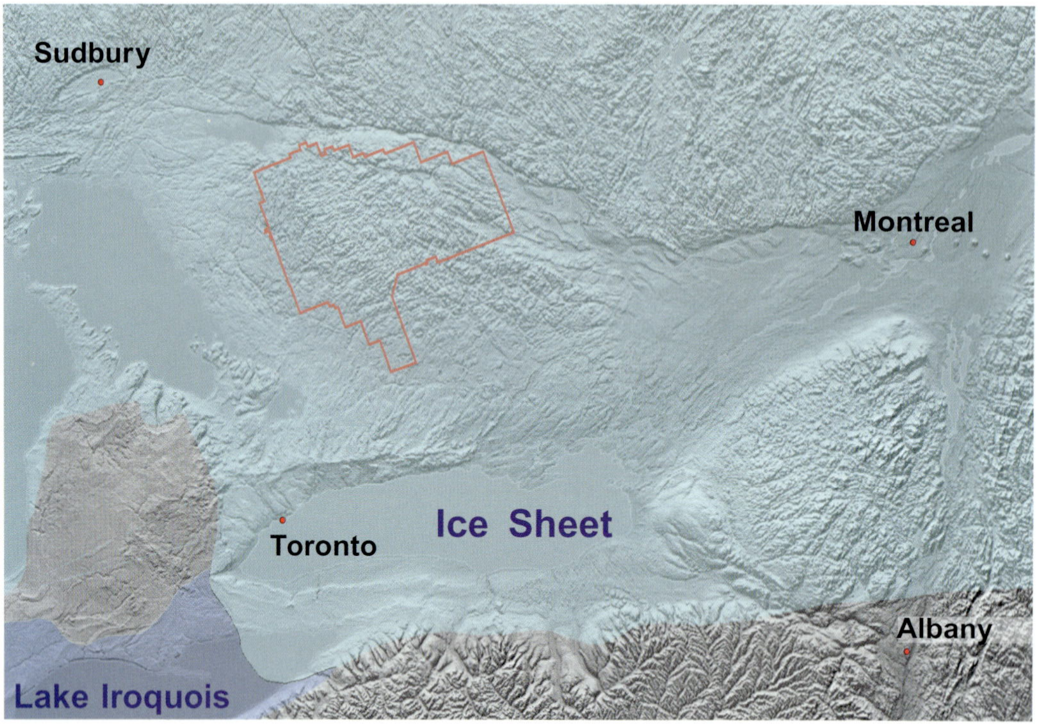

Illustrations on these two pages are adapted from Geology of Ontario, P.C. Thurston et al., Ontario Ministry of Northern Development and Mines, 1992.

11,800 years ago the ice retreated across Algonquin Park. The blue arrows show how the water was draining away. Lake Iroquois moved into the basin of today's Lake Ontario. A second great lake, Lake Algonquin, occupied the basin of today's Lake Huron. Lake Algonquin drained into Lake Iroqoois through a broad depression now occupied by the Kawartha Lakes. The water from Lake Algonquin and Lake Iroquois did an end run across the northern end of the Adirondack Mountains, through the depression now occupied by Lake Champlain, down the Hudson Valley, and into the Atlantic Ocean.

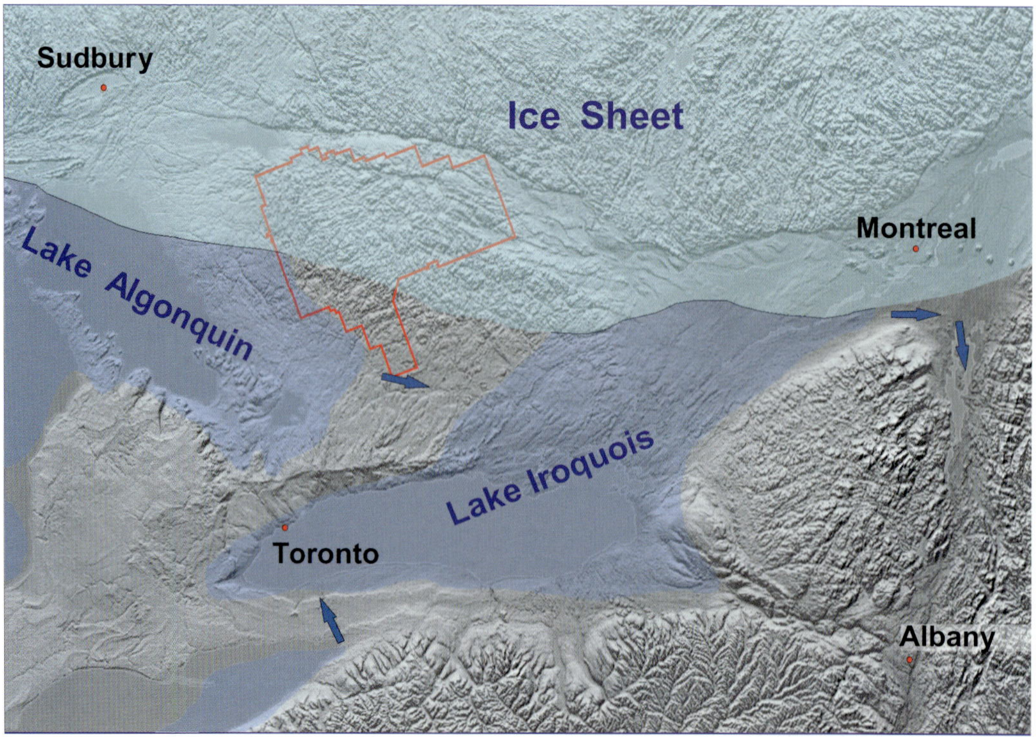

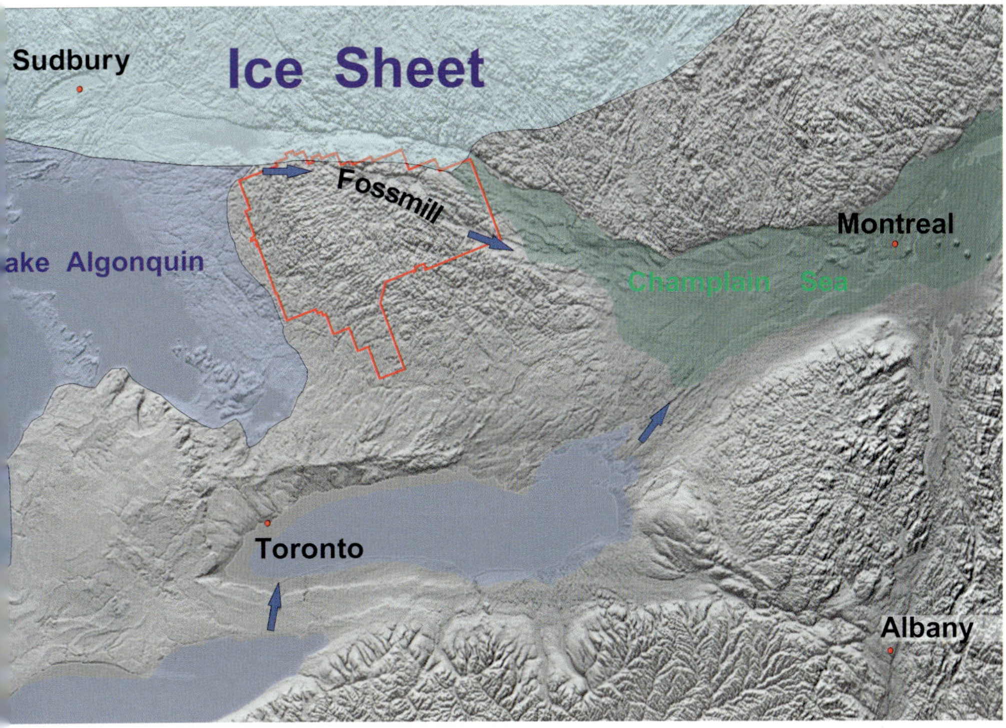

11,000 years ago the ice had retreated from Algonquin Park. The weight of the ice depressed the St. Lawrence and Ottawa river valleys below sea level. A long arm of the Atlantic Ocean, called the Champlain Sea, extended to Algonquin Park. During the 800 years or so that it took for the ice sheet to retreat across Algonquin, the meltwater from Lake Algonquin followed a number of channels to the Champlain Sea, including the Madawaska and the Bonnèchere valleys. The most impressive flow occurred along the Fossmill channel. This drainage channel opened suddenly, releasing a torrent of water across the northern part of Algonquin to the Barron Canyon and Petawawa River valleys. At its peak, this channel carried 1000 times the water now flowing over Niagara Falls. As this river widened and then flowed into the Champlain Sea it dropped huge volumes of sand that now favours pine forests.

A depressing concept

Remember how the lithosphere floats on the asthenosphere? Well, the weight of the continental ice caps was enough to depress the elevation of the ground under them. As the ice melted, the land began to rise again. This process is quite slow, because the asthenosphere is plastic, not liquid. Even today, Toronto is rising 2mm per year, while the shore of Hudson Bay is rising even faster.

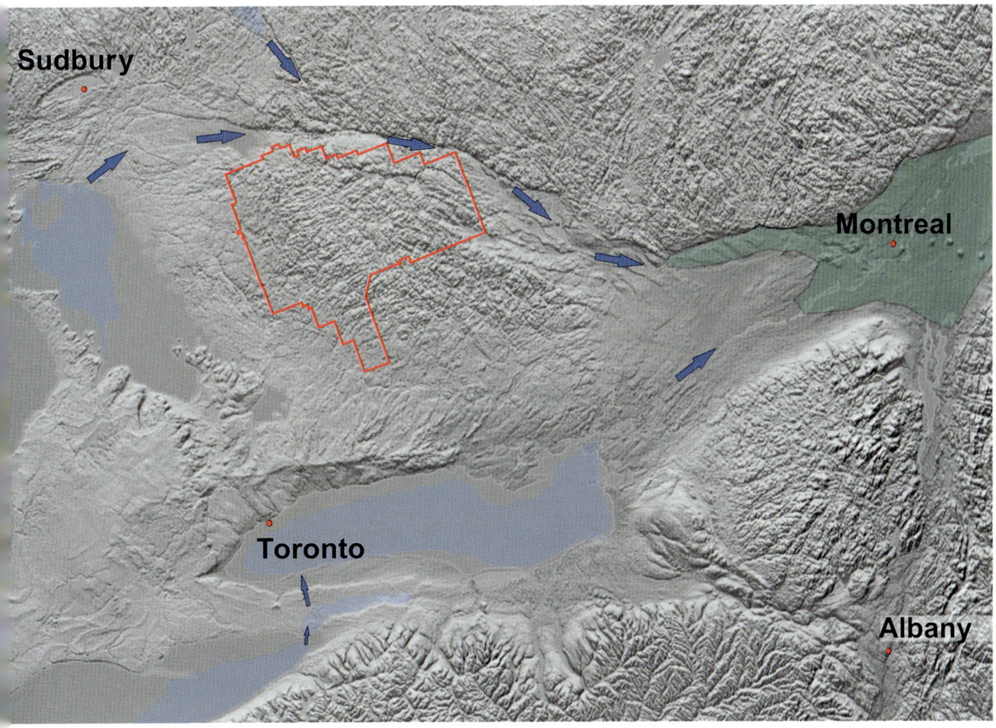

10,000 years ago the ice was gone from this part of the world. Released from its burden of ice, the lithosphere rose. The Champlain Sea retreated down the St. Lawrence Valley. The Great Lakes were smaller than today, because their outlet was closer to sea level. Since that time, they have become deeper and larger as their outlet along the St. Lawrence has continued to rise.

The legacy of ice

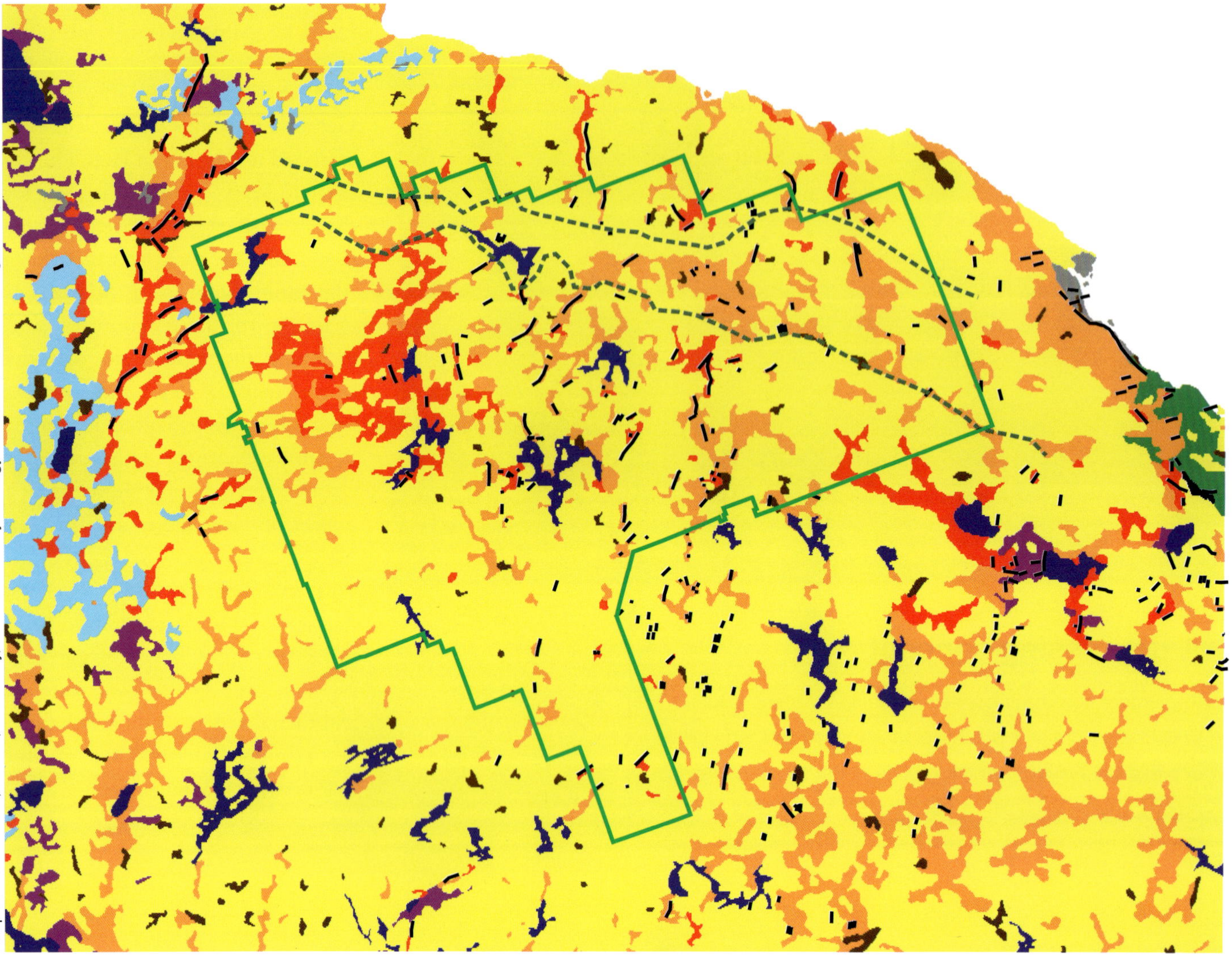

Adapted from Barnett, Cowan, and Henry, 1991 Quartenary Geology of Ontario, Ontario Geological Map 2555 and 2556.

Glacial deposits in and around Algonquin Park

Lakes
Glacial till
Ice contact deposits
Outwash deposits
Fine lacustrine deposits
Coarse lacustrine deposits
Marine deposits
Alluvium
Organic deposits
Eskers
Algonquin Park boundary
Fossmill drainage channel

Glacial deposits were the raw material that nature had to work with once the glaciers were gone and life was beginning to return. These deposits play an important role in determining the types of vegetation that will grow. This, in turn, has influenced development and settlement patterns. Let's take a look.

The map above shows the glacial deposits in and around Algonquin Park. We see a lot of yellow. This indicates areas covered with glacial till, which is unsorted debris that was simply deposited on the ground when the glacier melted. Glacial till contains minerals in all sizes: silt, clay, sand, pebbles, and boulders. It does not make good agricultural soil. The best agricultural soil forms in meltwater lakes: the lacustrine deposits, which are light blue and purple in our map. These areas lie outside of Algonquin to the west and northwest. Highway 11 courses through this area, following the settlement pattern in the better soil.

There is a large red area on the western side of Algonquin. This is an area with a large proportion of ice-contact deposits. These were formed where the glacial meltwater was trapped by the higher land to the east and south and could not flow away in rivers. Here we find the low rocky and gravely hills called moraines and kames. In contrast, the orange areas indicate outwash deposits. Note the Fossmill drainage channel that cuts across the northern part of Algonquin Park between the dashed green lines. This was a major channel for glacial meltwater for a few hundred years. As an immense river flowed eastward in this channel it slowed where the channel widens, dropping its load of sand on the northeastern part of Algonquin Park and along the shore of the Champlain Sea. The resulting sand plains are shown by the orange patches found between the dashed green lines and further east along the Ottawa River.

Further downstream on the Ottawa River we see the only green patch on this map. The water here was saltier, and marine deposits were formed.

Numerous eskers have been mapped in Algonquin Park, the short black lines on our map. Visitors to the interior can view some of these fascinating features along the Crow River west of Lake Lavieille and in Hogan Lake. The area west of Burntroot Lake provides excellent examples of eskers, kettle lakes, and kames.

When the ice disappeared it set the stage for a new beginning for Algonquin Park, one full of life, water, and change. The ice left a more subtle legacy than hills and lakes. We find that the ecosystems we recognize above the surface are directly related to the glacial debris hidden from sight below the surface.

See for yourself

While we could easily view samples of bedrock geology along Highway 60, it will require more effort to check out good examples of many glacial features in the park.

The easiest glacial features to see are the sand plains, which are **outwash deposits**. There is a large sand plain extending west of Lake of Two Rivers. The Lake of Two Rivers campground sits on this deposit; you can experience it tangibly when you drive your tent pegs into this nice sand. (If you were camping on glacial till, at least a few of your pegs would hit rocks and might have to be re-positioned). Walk the nearby Bat Lake Trail to experience the world on a sand plain. Visitors to the north end of the park can experience outwash deposits on the Berm Lake Trail, accessible from Achray.

Glacial till lies under your feet throughout much of Algonquin Park, but it is hard to see. Post 3 on the Bat Lake Trail and Post 3 on the Lookout Trail provide opportunities to see glacial till.

Visitors can see what it is like when a river drops part of its load as **alluvium** when it enters a lake. Current day examples include a large, shallow, flat area at the western end of Grand Lake. In the summer, this area sports an immense bed of waterlillies that is truly impressive if it is in bloom when you approach from the east. Smaller examples can be viewed where streams enter Carcajou and Rouge lakes.

If you are paddling along Grand Lake, check out the hill that rises from the south shore near the western end. There is a **meltwater channel** along here that was cut by water that was running between the hill that forms the south shore of Grand Lake and the ice that was sitting where Grand Lake is now.

While you are exploring Grand Lake, why not paddle into Carcajou Bay to enjoy the lovely grotto around the base of Carcajou Falls? Two short portages will take you to a steep-sided channel leading to Lower Spectacle Lake. The two Spectacle Lakes (you will immediately see how they got their name when you consult your map) are examples of **kettle lakes**, as is McDonald Lake, which is in the neighbourhood, but more difficult to reach.

Although there are numerous examples of **glacial erratics** throughout Algonquin, you can walk right up to one at Post 2 on the Lookout Trail. These are large boulders that were moved from far away by moving glaciers. The discovery of these "out of place" rocks was one of the first clues that led nineteenth-century geologists to realize that immense glaciers must have covered much of the northern hemisphere at some time in the past.

One of the best places to view **eskers** is from Hogan Lake. If you paddle toward the southern end from the north and keep an eye on the eastern shore, you should see a sequence of ridges that extend into the lake as blunt peninsulas. These are eskers. They do not look spectacular from lake level, so we have used computer graphics to show the shape of the land as you could see it from above.

Sitting in our canoe near the south end of Hogan Lake we might notice a number of bumps on the eastern shore. If we were in just the right position, we might see that one of the bumps is really a ridge.

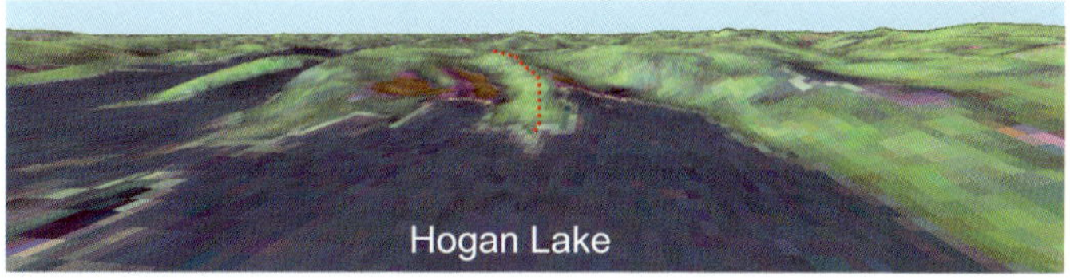

If we could magically rise up from our canoe, we could confirm that we are really seeing a curved ridge heading toward the east from shore, as shown by the red dotted line in this computer simulation of the view.

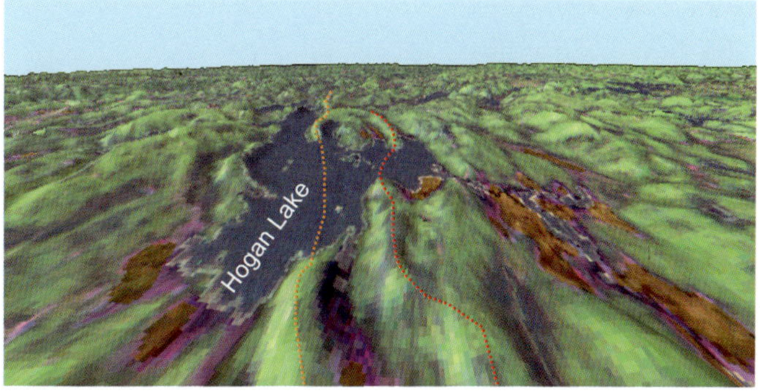

Rising farther and backing off, we would see that the ridge to the east also extends to the west on the other side of Hogan Lake. Several other ridges in the vicinity, such as the one marked in orange, would also become visible. These are eskers. Not much to look at from your canoe, but satellite imaging and computer graphics provide an overview that shows the long, sinuous shape characteristic of these glacial features.

Lush with life: Algonquin's ecology

Fast forward 10,000 years. The glaciers are gone; life is everywhere.

Plants and animals take advantage of their opportunities, adapt to their environment, and even alter the environment to make conditions more favourable for themselves. They create a living world moulded to their environment, something that lives and breathes like a super-organism. We call this an ecosystem.

Ecosytems evolve from a struggle for life. Millions of organisms compete for food to eat, space to grow, and opportunities to reproduce. Success involves intense competition, some cooperation, and plain luck. The energy to make this happen comes from the sun, so it is not surprising that climate plays a key role.

Climate: the harsh taskmaster

More than any other factor, climate determines what vegetation communities can grow successfully in a given area. Because of climate, the world is divided into zones with distinct types of vegetation. These zones are called biomes. Familiar examples include deserts, grasslands, and tropical rainforests.

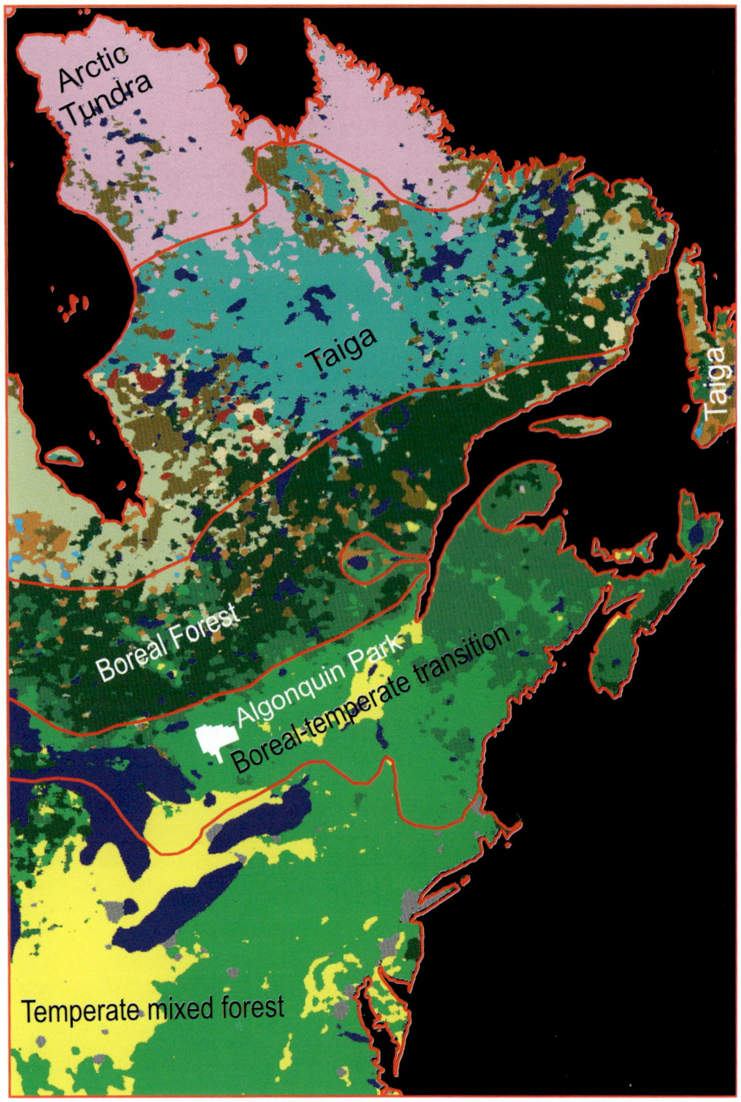

Vegetation cover data adapted from Global Land Cover 2000, courtesy Canada Centre for Remote Sensing

Legend for vegetation cover of northeastern North America

Forestland
- *Lichen woodlands*
- *Conifer forest, open canopy*
- *Conifer forest, closed canopy*
- *Mixedwood forest, closed canopy*
- *Mixedwood forest, open canopy*
- *Broadleaf deciduous forest*

Grassland and shrubland
- *Grassland with spase tree cover*
- *Tundra*
- *Shrubland*
- *Sparse vegetation*

Other
- *Inland water*
- *Cropland*
- *Mixed cropland and woodland*
- *Recently burned*
- *Urban*

The map presented here has been synthesized from several sources, particularly:

Natural Vegetation: North America, in Fullard, H. 1979, The Atlas of Canada and the World, George Philip Raintree Inc, Milwaukee, USA, p21; Scott, G. 1995. Canada's vegetation: a world perspective. McGill-Queen's University Press, Montreal; Raven, P. H., R. F. Evert, and S. E. Eichhorn, 1992. Biology of Plants, Fifth Edition, Worth Publishers, New York, USA, p 658; Brown, L., Grasslands, Alfred A. Knopf, New York, USA.

The map at left shows the biomes of northeastern North America, separated by red lines, and the types of vegetation that grow in each biome, indicated by colour.

In eastern North America precipitation is not a limiting factor; the biome zones are determined primarily by temperature. We find arctic tundra in northern Quebec. This is a land of low shrubs, grasses, and wildflowers that explode to life during a short growing season, and lie dormant the rest of the year. Moving south we begin to find open stands of small trees interspersed with lichens or mosses. We are crossing a transition zone to the boreal forest, sometimes called the taiga.

The boreal forest itself is characterized by large, closed stands of conifers, particularly spruces. The vegetation is a mosaic of patches, as seen on the map to the left. This is the legacy of fires that frequently burn here, leaving patches of different ages.

Algonquin Park lies in another transition zone, between the boreal forest and the temperate mixed forest. This location contributes to Algonquin's special nature. Depending on the local conditions, the forest may have a very boreal character, dominated by spruces and tamaracks, with some aspens and birches. Or it may seem much more southern, abounding in maples and oaks.

The temperate mixed forest farther south supports more species of trees than the forests to the north. In particular, maples, oaks, beeches, elms, and other broadleaf trees join the fray, each hunting for and defending niches where it and its progeny can thrive.

Algonquin's climate

The maps below show the two most important measures of the climate in and around Algonquin Park: temperature and precipitation.

The **temperature** is shown as growing degree days, a way of expressing the length and warmth of the growing season.

Note the blue blob that extends from the north down over Algonquin Park. It is definitely colder there! This is a result of the higher elevation of Algonquin's dome, because air cools as it is forced to rise over the dome. To the northeast, toward the Ottawa Valley, the elevation is lower and the climate is warmer.

The second map shows **precipitation**. Again, the higher elevation of Algonquin has an effect on its climate. As air masses move over Algonquin, usually from the west or northwest, the air must rise. It cools, forming clouds and rain or snow that falls on the western part of the park. When the air descends on the eastern side it is now drier, and there is less precipitation.

To summarize, the climate of Algonquin Park is cooler at higher elevations and warmer at lower elevations. It is wetter to the west and drier to the east. This has an important effect on the overall vegetation pattern: the warmer, drier eastern portion is more suitable for the growth of pine trees, while the moister portions to the west are more suitable for the growth of broadleaf trees and conifers that require more moisture. Within this general pattern there are many variations and exceptions. These result from additional, more subtle influences, as we shall see in the pages to come.

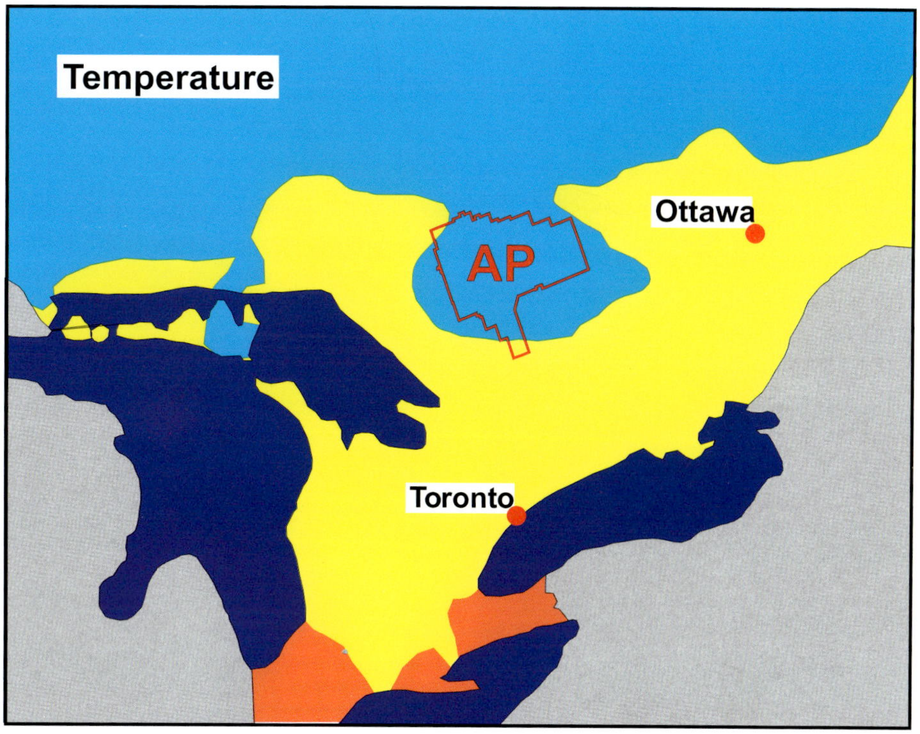

Average growing degree days, 1961-1990
1000-1500 1500-2000 2000-2500

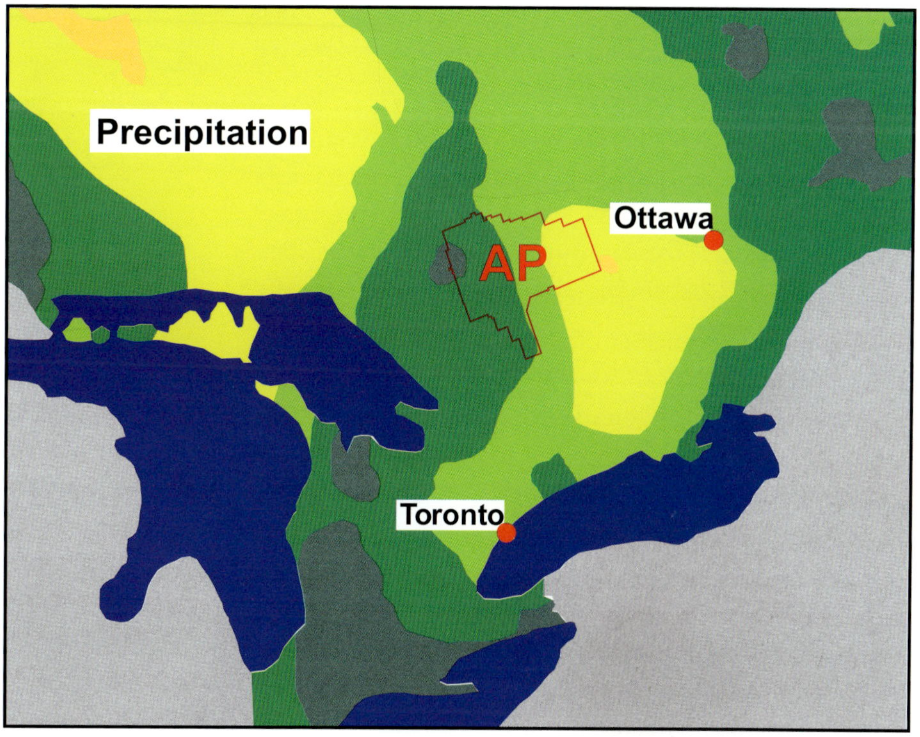

Precipitation during growing season, 1961-1990 (mm)
>600 550-600 500-550
450-500 400-450

The climate maps on this page were produced with the aid of interactive mapping tools provided by the Canadian Forest Service at http://www.glfc.cfs.nrcan.gc.ca/landscape/index_e.html. Details regarding the climate data used to produce these maps can be found in McKenney, D.W.; Kesteven, J.L.; Hutchinson, M.F.; Venier, L. 2001. Canada's plant hardiness zones revisited using modern climate interpolation techniques. Can. J. Plant Science. 81: 139-143.

The glaciers are gone — and life returns

When the glaciers retreated, they left behind rocks and glacial till – not much to support life. But life is tenacious, and before long lichens began growing on bare rocks, as they do today. Then mosses and lower plants established themselves on moister spots. Seeds of all sorts blew in on warm winds from the south. Some sprouted and took hold. Thus life began to build an ecosystem from a lifeless wasteland.

Soil, a mixture of minerals, organic matter, and varying amounts of air and water, is essential for an abundance of life on land. There was lots of water, but the soil was absent or impoverished. But life creates soil just as soil creates life, forming an upward spiral towards a richer future.

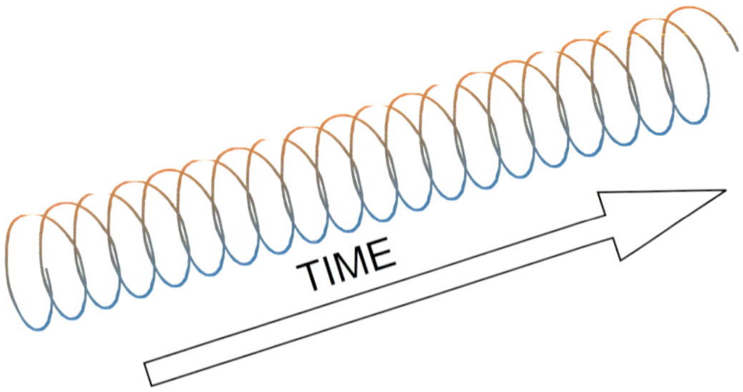

The spiral of soil and life. As soil formation processes go on, year after year after year, the soil becomes richer and deeper. It becomes able to support larger and more varied plants and animals.

Soil formation

How does this work? The diagram at right summarizes the major processes.

In **winter**, the living world is mostly asleep, but water freezes and thaws throughout the season and is a powerful force that literally breaks rocks apart.

Spring brings runoff from the winter snow. The water moves debris. It carries fine soil particles in small rivulets, and can even move sand, gravel, and rocks that find themselves in a stream during the spring torrent. As it percolates through the soil, water leaches soluble minerals deeper into the soil.

In **summer** life takes on a frenzied pace. Plants grow and their roots break rocks. Fungi break down dead plants and animals, adding organic matter to the soil. Soil animals, the unsung heroes of the soil-formation process, carry plant parts into the soil, loosening it, aerating it, and moving organic matter to deeper depths.

Fall deposits huge volumes of organic matter onto the soil surface. Trees shed leaves, twigs, and branches. Fall tempests fell entire trees, aided in some years by heavy wet snows.

By human standards, this process is painfully slow. Soil forms at rates ranging from 2 to 12 cm (about 1 to 5 inches) per century. That is why soil conservation is so important. With poor practices, we can degrade soil faster than nature can rebuild it.

Curtain call for the stars in the drama of soil formation. Millions upon millions of plants, animals, and microbes in the soil are the unsung heroes of life on Earth. Without them there would be no soil and no life on land.

Anatomy of a mature soil

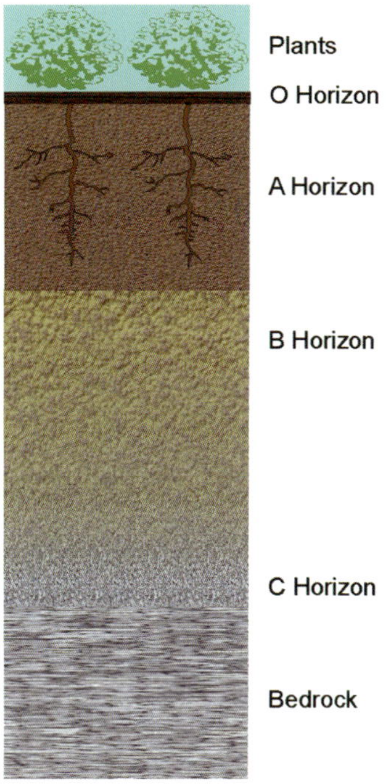

Mature soils consist of a number of distinct layers that soil scientists call "horizons". The illustration at left shows the major horizons of a mature soil. The top layer, the O horizon (for organic), consists of plant matter in the process of decomposition. Forests have a layer of dry litter on top: mostly leaves, together with sticks and branches. Digging down you will find wetter, increasingly decomposed organic matter. The brown soggy stuff right at the bottom of this layer is called humus.

Just below the humus is the A horizon. It consists of a mixture of fine organic matter, water, air and fragments of rocks. The sizes of the rock fragments determine the soil texture, which is described in terms of three principal components: sand, silt, and clay. For example loam, considered the best soil texture for agriculture, consists of about 50% sand, 30% silt, and 20% clay. Soil texture is strongly affected by the inorganic "parent material" that was present at the beginning of soil formation. In Algonquin Park, the parent material could be hard rocks or glacial deposits of till, gravel, sand, or silt. Till often contains larger rocks of all sizes that make it particularly difficult to farm. The organic matter gives the A horizon its characteristic brown colour, which is why darker soils are considered richer than lighter soils. The A horizon is the home of most soil life: small animals from millipede-size on down, as well as roots, fungi, bacteria, and other microbes.

The B horizon, or subsoil, contains much less life and organic matter. It is often called mineral soil. Chemicals are leached out of the A horizon and deposited in the B horizon as water percolates downward. Water carries finer soil particles downward, so the B horizon often has more clay and silt than the A horizon. The C horizon rests directly on top of the bedrock and contains larger rock fragments that are in the process of breaking up to become soil.

Soils through time: soil development

Four stages of soil development are shown at right. In the first stage a thin layer of glacial till rests on bedrock. Lichens, mosses, or other small plants colonize this layer. A thin A horizon begins to form under a very thin O horizon. This provides better water retention, and the C horizon begins to grow downward into the bedrock. As the A horizon grows thicker and richer from accumulation of organic matter, it can support larger plants and more soil animals. These increase the rate of growth of the A horizon. At the same time, water percolating through the A horizon begins to move minerals down, creating a young B horizon. After many centuries, a mature soil covers much of the landscape.

Soil can also be formed from other inorganic parent material such as sand and glacial till.

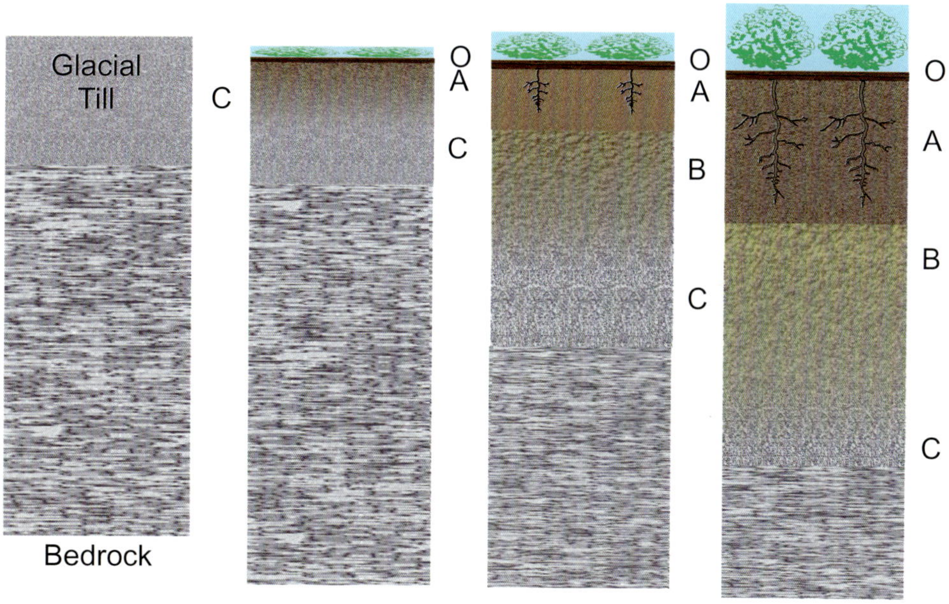

Soils through space: effects of topography

In Algonquin Park, the topography also influences soil formation. Because the bedrock is so hard, there may be no soil on exposed hilltops like those found near cliffs and lookouts. Near the crest, but in less-exposed locations, a thin layer of soil can be found supporting small plants. Farther down the slope, the soil may still be thin, but it can support tall but shallow-rooted trees. The best soils are found in well-drained areas near the bottoms of hills. In poorly-drained areas that are just above the water table for most of the year, growing conditions are more difficult. Fewer types of plants can inhabit these areas. Finally, in wetlands thick deposits of poorly-decomposed organic matter accumulate, creating organic soils where the O horizon dominates.

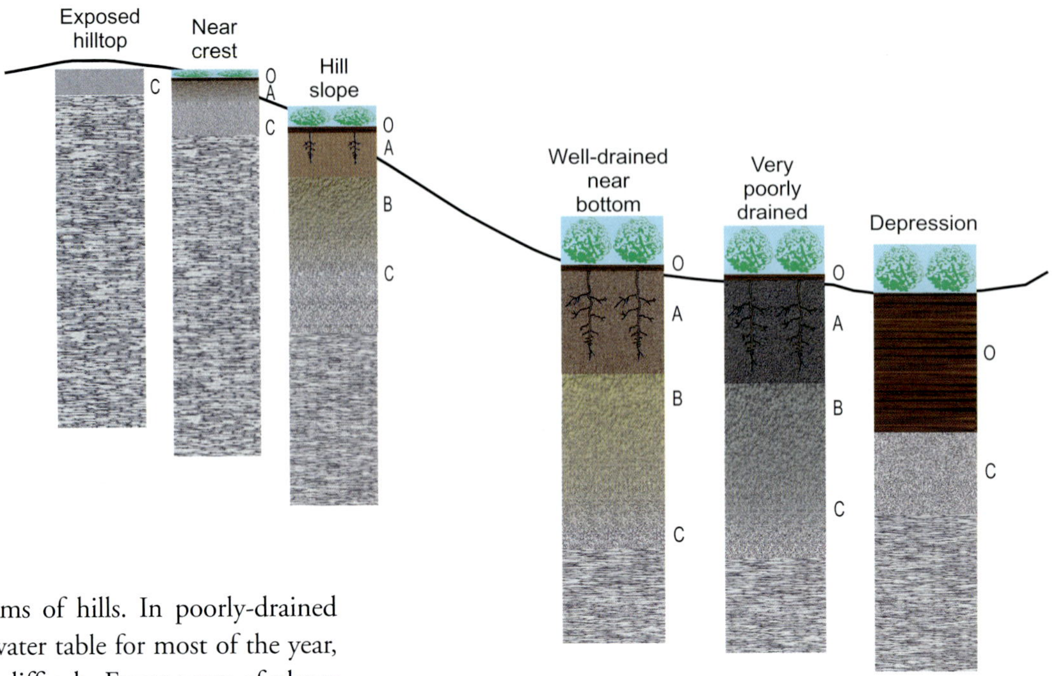

The type of soil influences the type of plants that can grow on it. Over time, the types of plants also affect the soil. For example, the plant litter from conifers makes the soil more acid, favouring these trees over broadleaf trees.

What a site!

We have seen how soils develop over time and space. Their parent material and drainage determine how fertile they are, and how well they retain moisture. Fertility and moisture, in turn, play a major role in determining which kinds of plants will grow in a particular area. Scientists call an area with particular fertility, moisture and characteristic plants a "site." The plants of a site form groups called plant communities.

Small changes in topography determine whether rainfall and snowmelt run off quickly (drier sites) or linger in ponds and puddles (moister sites). Sandy soils promote drier sites, while finer soils that retain moisture promote moister sites. Fertility depends on the soil's texture and chemistry. The diagram at right shows how tree species adapt to particular sites. Note how the conifers populate the left side of the graph, indicating that they are better adapted to poor fertility than the broadleaf trees. Some species are restricted to a narrow range of site conditions. For example, tamarack is almost always found in poor wet sites, while beech is found in a small range of drier, richer sites. These are called indicator species, because their presence points to a specific kind of site. The diagram is divided into five vegetation associations that are tinted to match the drawings on the next page.

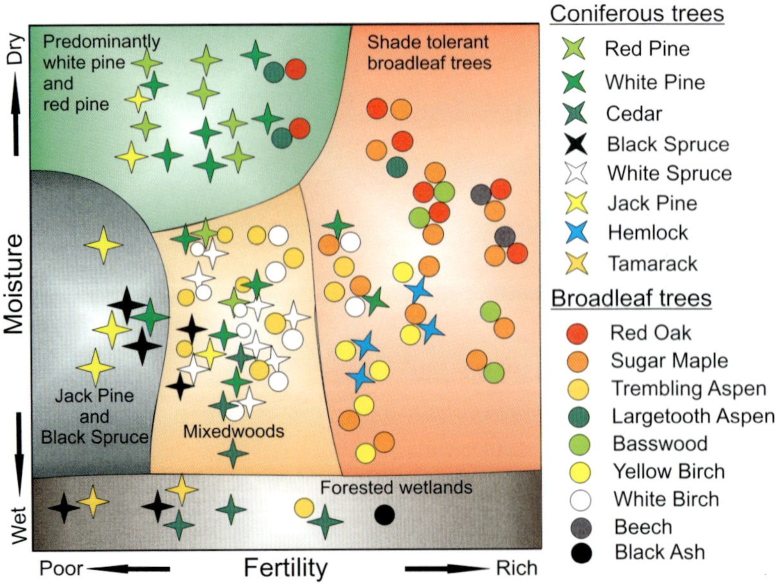

Adapted from "Field Guide to Forest Ecosystems of Central Ontario", by Chambers, Naylor, Nieppola, Merchant, and Uhlig, 1997. Available through the Friends of Algonquin Park, Box 248, Whitney, Ontario K0J 2M0.

Algonquin sites

Two zones, uplands and lowlands, characterize the types of sites found in Algonquin Park. The uplands rise to the west and south, while the lowlands lie to the north and east. From a general perspective, the soils and vegetation are distinctly different. The lowland soils are much more sandy because they are glacial deposits with their silt and clay washed away by glacial meltwater. They are much drier, because the temperature is warmer, there is less precipitation, and because water drains more quickly from sandy soil. They support large stands of red and white pine, trees that are well adapted to frequent dry conditions. The upland soils receive more precipitation and hold their moisture better, so they support a wider selection of trees, particularly broadleaf varieties. Within each of these two areas, site conditions can vary, producing a rich mix of plant communities.

The diagrams below, called topographic profiles, are an idealized representation that shows how soil moisture and fertility vary from hilltop to valley bottom, and how the dominant trees vary in response.

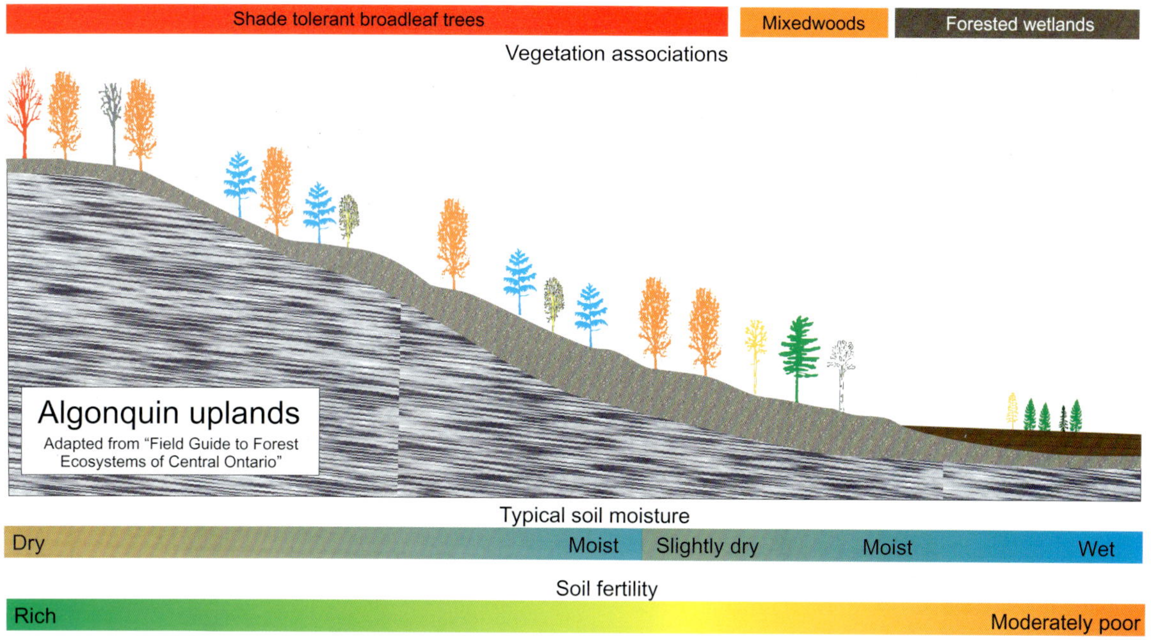

Most of the western portions of Algonquin Park are uplands where the soil parent material is glacial till. Sugar maples blanket the hilltops and slopes except in the driest sites, which are occupied by oaks. The lower slopes are occupied by mixedwoods. Pockets of hemlocks can be found in wet depressions on the hillsides, while conifers occupy the valleys and fringe the lakeshores.

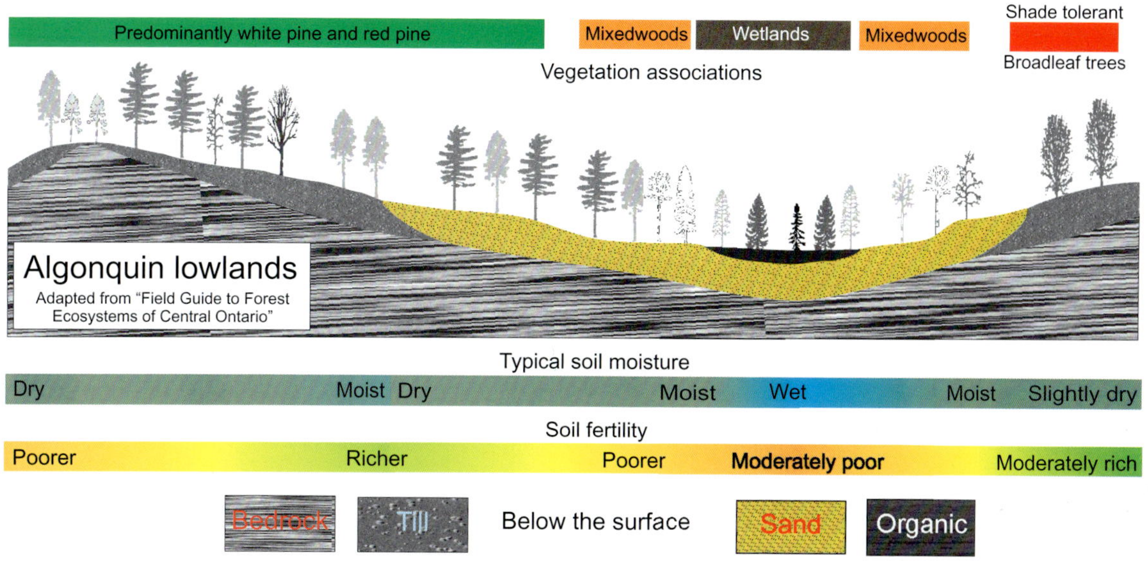

Much of the eastern portions of Algonquin Park are lowlands where the soil parent material is sand. White and red pines form large stands in the sandy areas. Mixedwoods and broadleaf stands are found where moisture and fertility permit.

Land cover map

By comparing topography (page 10), glacial deposits (page 22), and land cover (below), we note some important characteristics:

1. A predominance of broadleaf trees at higher elevations and in the south and west.
2. A predominance of conifers at lower elevations and in the north and east.
3. A mixed forest, dominated by broadleaf trees, occupies intermediate elevations.
4. Dense conifers are generally found on outwash deposits.
5. The agricultural area to the northwest, outside the park, is located on lacustrine deposits. These produce better soils for agriculture.
6. Poorly drained areas with bogs and fens dot both uplands and lowlands.

Algonquin Park Museum

A real-world topographic profile. Note the red and orange sugar maples that indicate the broadleaf communities and the green conifers fringing the lakes. A dark green hemlock stand inhabits a moist site just left of centre.

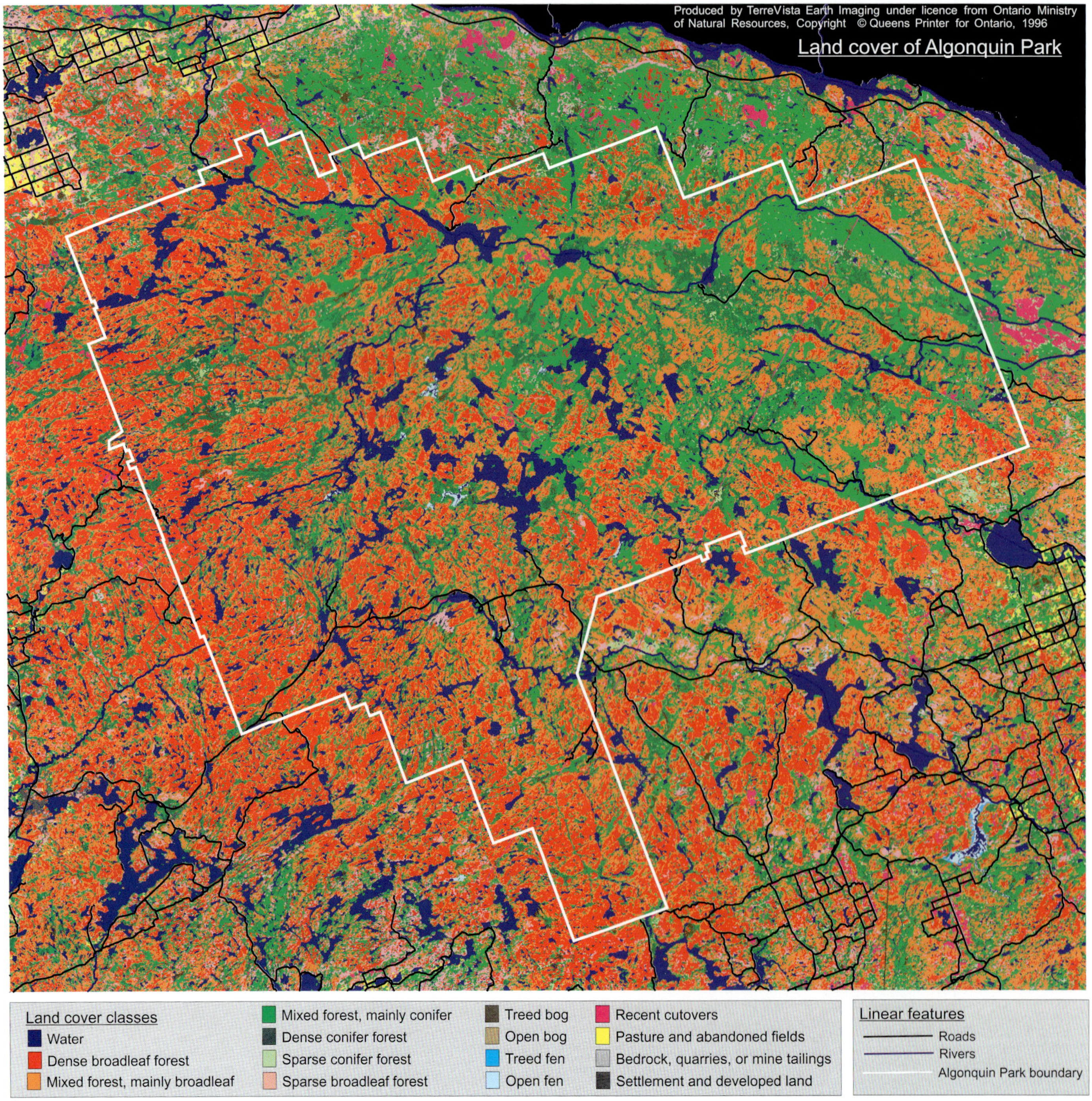

The biosphere — the layer of life

We have been examining the biosphere, the layer of life that coats parts of our planet like a very thin film. How thin? Well, if the earth were the size of an apple, the atmosphere would be its skin. The thickest parts of the biosphere are 1000 times thinner. The biosphere — where all life exists — is a wispy-thin film on our planet.

Within the biosphere, plant life in forests is organized into layers. From top to bottom, we find trees, shrubs, herbs, mosses, and fungi.

Algonquin Park Museum

The white pine (left), together with the red pine, are the most common trees on Algonquin's drier sites. Sugar maples (right) produce a riot of colour in the fall.

Layers of life

Trees make the forest. In a mature stand, they form a closed canopy, like an umbrella over the forest floor, and intercept most of the incoming sunlight. They grow trunks and branches by combining energy from the sun with carbon dioxide from the air and water and nutrients collected by their roots. They give the forest its structure, form, and colour. They provide habitat for other plants, birds, mammals, reptiles, amphibians, as well as innumerable invertebrates.

Shrubs and saplings form what foresters call the understory, where they struggle to survive in the dim sunlight under the canopy. When a mature tree dies or a group of trees fall down, saplings make a frenzied rush to fill the gap. Only a few will make it.

Herbs are smaller plants. They do not produce woody stems or branches. They often emerge, bloom, and reproduce in the spring, before the canopy trees leaf out. In very dense canopies, there may be so little sunlight that the shrub layer and the herb layer are absent.

Mosses are non-vascular plants: they do not have water-carrying tubes (technically vascular tissue), so they are mostly found in wet areas.

Fungi play an essential role as the decomposers of the biosphere. The top 20 cm (8") of soil may contain 5 tonnes of fungi and bacteria in every hectare (2.5 acres) of forest. About 80% of vascular plants in the forest form mutually beneficial associations between their roots and fungi intertwined around and between them, playing a crucial role in plant nutrition. This association makes our trees more resistant to harsh conditions.

Saplings: maple and balsam fir

Shrubs: blueberry and Labrador tea

Bunchberry

Horsetail

Lily of the valley

Bracken fern

Moss-covered log

Moss forest floor in a spruce bog

Sphagnum in a peat bog

Algonquin Park Museum

Fungi exist primarily as mycelium (left), but pop up as mushrooms to reproduce.

Plant ecology

To live and grow, organisms need space, energy and nutrients, and they need to reproduce. Their numbers increase through successful reproduction. This leads to competition and depletion of resources, limiting their numbers. So one of the most fundamental considerations in ecology is the production and consumption of resources.

Nearly all plants have a unique advantage in the competition for life: chlorophyll. This enables them to obtain the energy they need from the sun. But this makes sunlight a precious resource, and the competition for it can be fierce. Being immobile, plants are totally subject to the vagaries of the spot where they grow and are at the mercy of predators great and small.

To prosper, plants have evolved a remarkable array of strategies. Some have seeds that lie dormant for decades and then grow quickly when conditions are opportune. Some have remarkable persistence, capable of languishing for years in the shade of taller trees until a gap appears when one or more of the canopy trees die. Some have evolved to live and even thrive in extreme habitats such as nutrient-poor acid bogs. Many plants employ chemicals to keep insects and other predators at bay. They may also engage in chemical warfare against each other. Most plants have prolific reproductive ability to ensure that at least a few of their progeny find a favourable location to grow and continue the species. Think of the huge number of airborne seeds produced by dandelions, milkweeds, and maples. Other plants enclose their seeds in a nutritious package to encourage animals to carry them away. Many plants propagate themselves asexually in addition to proliferating through seeds. In Algonquin Park, this is perhaps most dramatic for the poplars, particularly trembling aspen. Here and there we can find aspen groves where hundreds of seemingly individual trees are all clones sprouting from a single underground root system.

Can we observe ecology in action? Yes, we can, through the process called natural succession.

Ecology in action: natural succession

In forests, natural succession begins and ends with a disturbance. A cataclysmic disturbance could be a devastating fire, clearcut logging, or conversion of the forest to a farm. At the end of this disturbance, nature reclaims the land. Grasses and herbs quickly take over. We often call these "pioneer" species weeds. Soon more attractive wildflowers become established, followed by shrubs and saplings. As succession progresses, the species that do best will be those best adapted to the conditions of the site. The first forest to appear will be composed of fast-growing trees intolerant to shade such as pin cherries, birches and poplars. Over the decades, the patient maples, oaks, and beeches will invade the understory and eventually replace the shorter-lived poplars and birches. If there is no new disturbance, the forest grows into ripe old age. Old-growth forests contain large old trees, many of which are beginning to deteriorate and some of which are already dead. The forest floor is littered with the trunks of fallen trees from years and decades past.

Because Algonquin Park is protected from fire, clearcut logging, and agricultural development, it may be a long time indeed before another cataclysmic disturbance resets the successional clock. But local disturbances happen all the time. Storms knock down patches or swaths of trees. Beavers flood an area for a few years. These disturbances return parts of the forest to the shrub and sapling stage of succession, and the process starts afresh.

Pine forests have a simpler path of succession. We have seen that they often have a competitive advantage on sandy soils. They also "like" forest fires. Their cones can survive fires. In fact, jack pine cones depend on fire to open and release their seeds. And mature pines have pitch and resin that make forest fires more intense, destroying the competition and preparing the way for the next generation.

Chance also plays a role. While the good sites on the western highlands of Algonquin generally grow into sugar maple stands in the long term, there are pine stands here as well. These are believed to have been established after rare but intense forest fires that burned these areas in previous centuries.

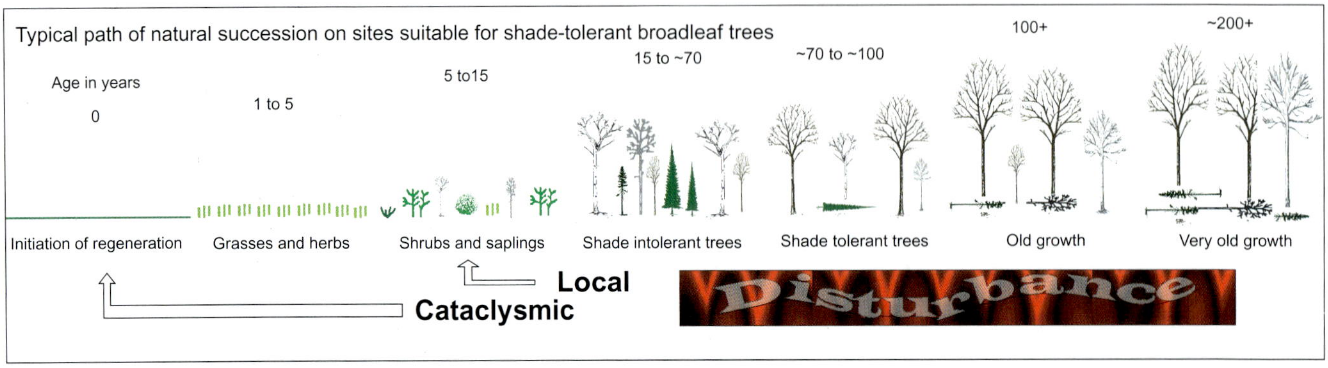

See for yourself

There are ample opportunities to see plant ecology in Algonquin Park. We have prepared the table below as a quick guide to the most accessible, interesting, and informative locations for observing the ecology of plant communities. But everywhere you go you can observe plant ecology in action, once you know what to look for.

What to see	Where to see it	Significance
Big white pines	Big Pines Trail; Berm Lake Trail, Post 3; side trail off Crow River	See big white pines and learn about their ecology.
Biggest white pines	Big Crow reserve and Dividing Lake area	Examples of the very large white pines in hardwood stands as they appeared before most were harvested in the 1800s.
Pine stand on sandy soil	Bat Lake Trail, Post 2; Berm Lake trail	Example of the conditions favouring pine found much more commonly on east side.
Pine stand in hardwood area	Big Pines Trail, Post 3; Hardwood Lookout Trail, Post 3	Special circumstances (like an opening from fire) must have existed to get these trees established.
White pine ecology	Berm Lake Trail	The roles of soil and fire; birds and mammals associated with pine stands.
Sugar maple stand	Hardwood Lookout Trail, Post 1; 2	Specific requirements for hardwoods (broadleaf trees); shade tolerance; absence of flowers except before leaf-out.
Succession following farming	Booth's Rock Trail, Post 4	See how much has grown back even on land that was cleared for a farm.
Plant succession	Two Rivers Trail, Post 6	See the pioneer overstory and second growth understory.
Post-fire succession by aspen	North shore of north arm of Lake Opeongo	Trembling aspen is a typical post-fire pioneer species. The fire occurred in 1953. A fifty-year-old aspen stand is reaching maturity.
Beaver meadow	Beaver Pond Trail, Post 9; Mizzy Lake Trail, Post 11	Beaver meadows represent an early stage of natural succession.
Blowdown	Two Rivers Trail, Post 9	Blowdown as a disturbance agent that initiates a new round of natural succession.
Decay	Hardwood Lookout Trail, Post 7	Importance of fungi in breaking down dead things and recycling nutrients.
Hemlock stand on a moister site	Bat Lake Trail, Post 7; Hardwood Lookout Trail, Post 5; Booth's Rock Trail, Post 2	Special requirements of hemlock; associated birds (e.g., blackburnian warbler; Black-throated green warbler), and deer.
Yellow birch	Hemlock Bluff Trail, Post 3; Hardwood Lookout Trail, Post 4	Special conditions needed to establish yellow birch.
Red pine	Dickson Lake	Oldest trees in the park: 340 years.
Red spruce	Hardwood Lookout Trail, Post 11	Special site requirements of red spruce.
Boreal-temperate contrast	Mizzy Lake Trail, Post 12	Typical northern (boreal forest) and typical southern (temperate forest) communities growing within a short distance; example of site.
Peat bog	Spruce bog boardwalk; Bat Lake Trail, Post 8	Special ecology of bogs.
Alders	Bat Lake Trail, Post 8	Nitrogen fixing plant.
What is wilderness?	Booth's Rock Trail, Post 7	An opportunity to contemplate whether Algonquin is or is not wilderness.

A beaver meadow represents the beginning of forest succession.

Algonquin Park Museum

Inside a young stand of broadleaf trees with a forest floor covered with shade-tolerant plants.

Bogs: a study in adaptation

Bogs are different and fascinating. Conditions in bogs are so unusual that highly specialized plants live there. Bogs form as a succession of stages in areas where water collects but moves slowly (some beaver ponds) or not at all (kettles). Initially, common plants like cattails and water lilies colonize the shoreline. Then more specialized plants such as a particular sedge called *Carex lasiocarpa* start to form floating mats that slowly spread from the edge toward the centre. As these mats get established, they grow thicker toward the shore, and a wider variety of plants grow on them. Eventually the mats cover the water entirely (kettles) or just allow a narrow stream to flow through. The water under the mat of plants becomes more and more acid and depleted of nutrients, preventing the dead plant matter that falls from its underside from decaying. The plant matter accumulates and becomes peat. Sphagnum ("peat moss") and other plants that can tolerate the acid, nutrient poor environment become the principal inhabitants toward the centre of the bog mat. Near the edges, as the peat accumulates, tamarack and then black spruce can become established. The environment toward the centre of a bog is so poor in nutrients that some plants (pitcher plants and sundews in Algonquin Park) have resorted to catching and digesting insects.

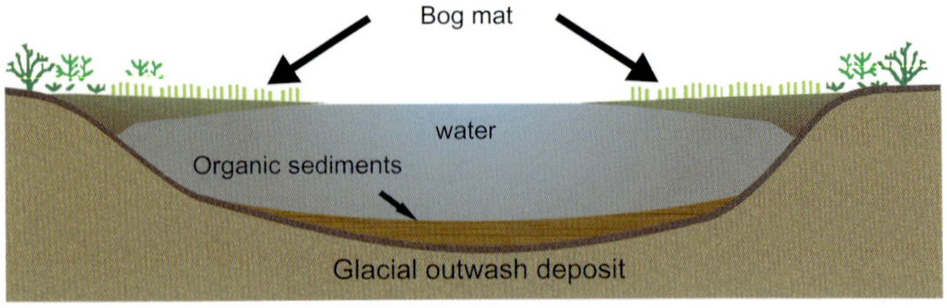

The early stages of bog development. The bog mat is growing toward the centre of the pond, and organic sediments are collecting at the bottom.

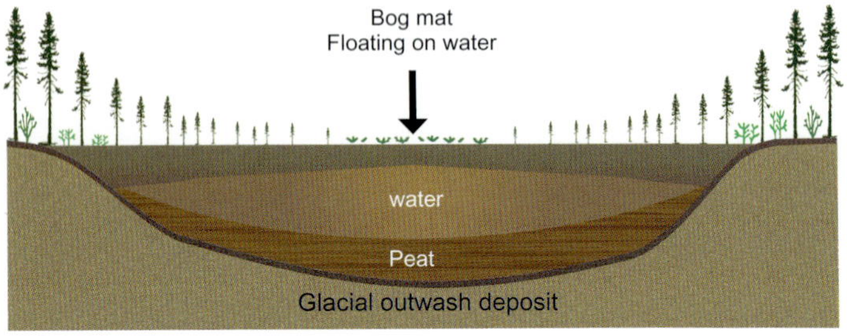

The late stages of bog development. The bog mat has covered (or nearly covered) the water. Peat is accumulating at the bottom. The water is brown and acid from chemicals leaching from the dead plants, which decay very slowly from lack of oxygen in the water. Spruce trees border the bog, thick and healthy at the shore and sparser and stunted toward the centre because of increasingly poor growing conditions.

Algonquin Park Museum

A typical kettle bog. Note how the black spruce trees decrease in size toward the centre. Inside the zone where black spruce can grow there are additional zones of vegetation indicated by different colours.

Labrador tea, a common low shrub found in bogs and other wet areas.

A mature bog mat growing toward the stream from both sides. Note the decreasing vigour of the black spruce toward the stream. This bog can be viewed nicely from the observing platform at the Visitor Centre.

Algonquin Park Museum

Birders come from far and wide to search for the spruce grouse, which inhabits Algonquin's bogs.

Algonquin Park Museum

Inside the black spruce stand at the edge of a bog one finds mosses and horsetails covering the forest floor.

Animal ecology

Animals have two things that plants do not: brains and mobility. They can sense danger, find food and mates, and move their bodies to get what they want and avoid what they don't want. This makes animal ecology much more complicated than plant ecology, but for many, more fascinating.

Food chains and pyramids

Every living thing needs energy. For green plants, this means sunlight. For animals, this means FOOD. The diagram at right shows the **food chain**, one of the fundamental concepts in ecology. Green plants are the primary producers. They make their own food by storing chemical energy as sugars and starches.

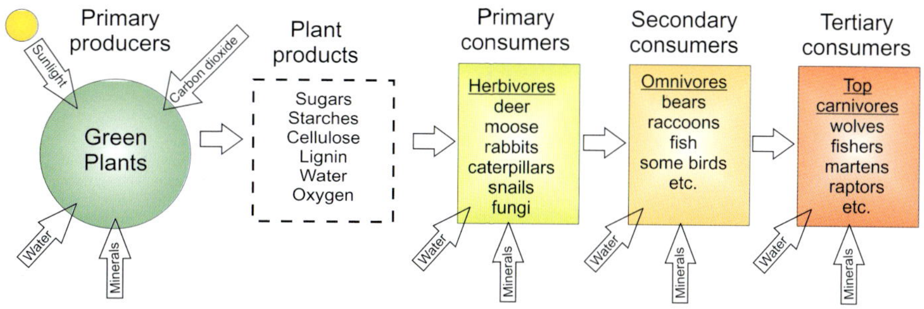

An army of herbivores of all sizes, from moose to microbes, consume these plants. The fungi specialize in breaking down plant and animal matter using a vast pharmacy of high-powered enzymes. Further down the food chain are the omnivores and carnivores. These are the animals of greatest interest to many visitors.

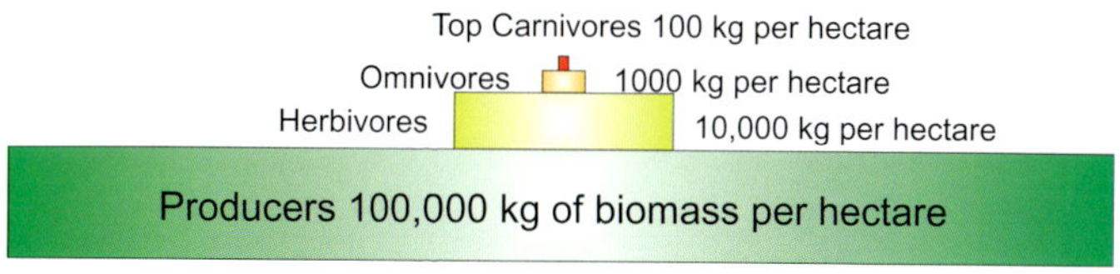

The food chain is not very efficient. Photosynthesis turns only one to two per cent of the sunlight falling on plants into chemical energy, compared to the 15-20 per cent efficiency of solar cells, for example. Moving down the food chain, creatures use only about 10 per cent of what they consume. This means that a tremendous amount of living matter must be available to support the higher stages in the food chain. Look at the little squat pyramid above. Each rectangle represents the weight of living matter in a hectare (2.5 acres) of land. Top carnivores, the tiny red cherry on top, require the entire ecosystem to support them. The wolves, raptors, and game fish that attract us to Algonquin Park prove that the area sports a fully-functioning ecosystem.

Of mice and moose

The drawing at right illustrates the food pyramid most dramatically. The size of each animal appears in proportion to their total weight per hectare in Algonquin Park. Because they are so abundant, the mouse is drawn as big as a moose. The bear and wolves are tiny because the ecosystem can only support small numbers of them. The biggest surprise may be the caterpillar. Caterpillars can build up huge populations by living near the bottom of the food pyramid. Of course, this makes them an abundant food source for the next level higher on the pyramid.

Howard Coneybeare and AP Museum

Populations, predators, prey, parasites, and people

A lot of visitors come to Algonquin worried whether the animals (usually meaning mammals) are "ok"... whether they have healthy populations. This is an easy question to ask and a very difficult one to answer.

First, we have to recognize that in nature, a healthy population may be a fluctuating population. Hudson's Bay Company recorded purchases of pelts of snowshoe hare and lynx across North America from 1821 to 1934. These records reveal a remarkable population cycle. The populations of the snowshoe hare climbed, crashed, and then rebuilt in a cycle that repeated every ten years, give or take a year or two, throughout the entire period. The lynx populations show the same pattern, but delayed by about a year. In Algonquin the snowshoe hare populations fluctuate, but less dramatically, and the lynx is rare if not absent.

Algonquin's deer, moose, and wolves have experienced dramatic changes in the past 100 years. Careful studies into changes in their populations have revealed important insights into the complexities of nature. We have learned to be very cautious about intervening, because the results are often quite different than expected.

During the first half of the twentieth century conditions were very favourable for the white-tailed deer, an immigrant to Algonquin from the south. Large areas of shrubs and young forest were at the early stages of natural succession (see page 32) following large-scale logging and associated activities. Even larger areas were recovering from forest fires. These areas provide abundant food supplies for deer, who browse on new shoots. They flourished, reaching peaks estimated at 30,000 to 100,000 animals within the park. Moose populations, in contrast, were quite low. Then industrial activity was cut back and fire suppression improved, allowing the forest to mature. This reduced the amount of food for the deer and their populations gradually declined. Moose populations began to increase. Why? Scientists found that the deer harbour a brain worm that does not seem to harm them, but is passed to moose and is lethal to them. Fewer deer result in more healthy moose.

During the same time, park authorities put a lot of effort into trying to manage wolf populations. At first, wolves were considered "vermin" to be shot, trapped, and poisoned. The abundant deer populations kept the wolves well fed and they could replace their losses. As understanding of the natural world grew, persecution of wolves was replaced by protection. But their numbers have not increased dramatically because of the gradual decline in deer populations. In fact, Algonquin's wolves have to travel outside the park in the winter to find deer where there is a larger proportion of shrubs and young forest.

Habitat

Research during the past century has shown that, in many cases, the most effective way to promote healthy animal populations is to ensure they have adequate habitat.

Habitat comprises the places animals need for food and shelter. The diagram at right shows the habitat requirements of four featured species in Algonquin: moose, deer, pileated woodpeckers, and red-shouldered hawks. Note how the pileated woodpecker can exist in many of the different types of forests found in Algonquin. It does not have specialized habitat requirements. Red-shouldered hawks, on the other hand, are limited to shade tolerant broadleaf stands on sites that have intermediate moisture, not too wet and not too dry. This raptor has specialized habitat requirements. Note also how the moose and deer have different requirements at different times of year. The moose, in particular, require wetlands in summer. Without these wetlands, there probably would not be moose. Understanding and protecting habitat is the first step toward ensuring healthy animal populations.

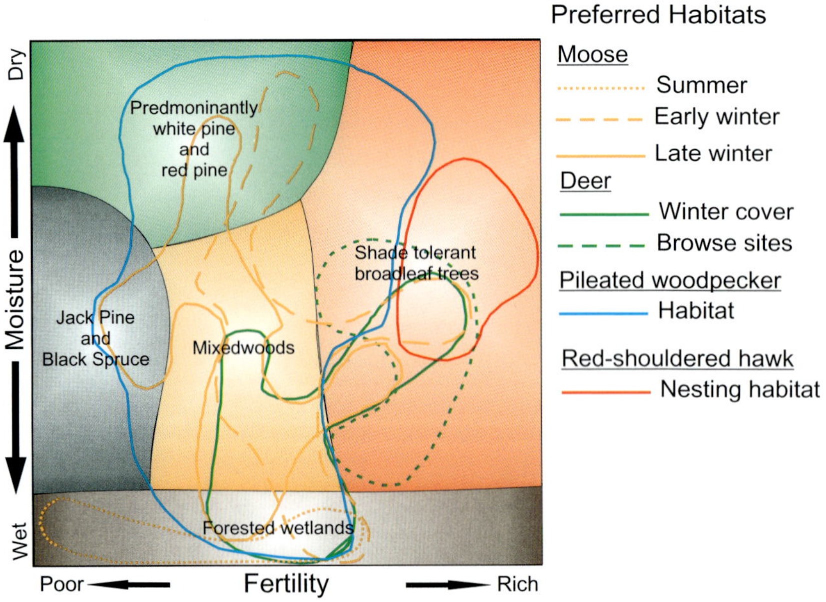

Adapted from "Field Guide to Forest Ecosystems of Central Ontario", by Chambers, Naylor, Nieppola, Merchant, and Uhlig, 1997. Available through the Friends of Algonquin Park, Box 248, Whitney, Ontario K0J 2M0

Lake ecology

Algonquin's lakes are central to its appeal. For visitors they enhance the scenery and provide opportunities for swimming, fishing, and canoeing. For their inhabitants they present an ecosystem that is quite different from those found on land.

As on land, lakes have a food chain based on green plants as the primary producers. "Traditional" plants, with leaves, stems, and roots, can only live in the shallow water near shore.

Though the rest of the lake may seem devoid of plant life, it is not. Millions of algae, of many different kinds, float in the water. For them, however, the necessities of life are much scarcer than for their land-based cousins. Take sunlight, for example. It is partially reflected away at the surface and then strongly absorbed once it gets into the water. Algae must live near the surface to get enough sunshine.

On land, plants use their roots to absorb essential nutrients such as potassium, calcium, phosphorus, and nitrogen. Algae must find what they need dissolved in the water. The nutrient richness of the water is a key factor that determines how much life, and what kind of life, a lake has.

Algonquin's lakes are mostly low to medium in nutrients. In the highlands, the catchment basin surrounding many lakes is small, the rocks are not rich in the most important minerals, and they weather slowly. All of these factors add up to lakes with low nutrient levels. In the lowlands the situation is only a bit better. The primary biological productivity, the amount of plant matter produced in Algonquin lakes, is therefore relatively low. Since plants form the base of the food pyramid (see page 35), and they are limited by nutrients, the entire pyramid is smaller. According to its trail guide, Peck Lake can only produce about 300 grams of trout per hectare (2.5 acres) per year. No wonder everyone is concerned about over-fishing!

Many of the primary producers and primary consumers in a lake are microscopic: algae and weird and wonderful tiny animals that feed on them. There is also a large variety of small animals: snails, crayfish, insect larvae and nymphs (immature adults), and tadpoles, for example. The algae and small animals support schools of minnows which in turn support larger fish such as perch, pumpkinseed (sunfish), and trout. At the top of the food chain are birds (loons, kingfishers, herons, ospreys, mergansers) and people. The relatively low productivity at the base of Algonquin's food pyramid means that the larger aquatic birds do not have high populations, and fishing by humans must be controlled. Nonetheless, most lakes support at least one loon family, canoeists have a good chance of spotting a great blue heron if they paddle quietly in and around shallow waters, and everyone is allowed to try to catch a few fish.

Algonquin Park Museum

There is a lot going on beneath the surface of this seemingly tranquil lake.

While nutrients limit plants, oxygen can be a constraint for animals. We land animals take oxygen for granted, being bathed in it by our atmosphere. Fish, amphibians, and lower animals must obtain oxygen dissolved in the water, which is in much shorter supply. In fact, oxygen is the ultimate limit on the productivity of a lake. If a lake is fertilized, either deliberately or inadvertently (through runoff from farms, for example), the plant productivity can explode as algae "blooms" and produce too much dead organic matter whose decomposition uses up the oxygen. The enhanced plant productivity ends up choking off the rest of the food pyramid.

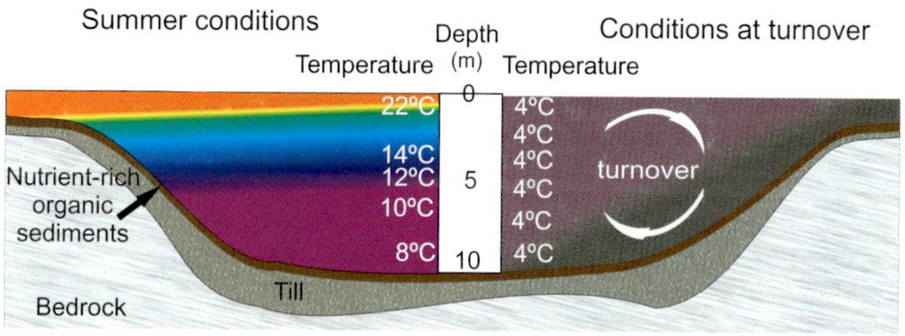

Algonquin's lakes, as well as myriads of other lakes on the Canadian Shield, go through a seasonal cycle that boosts their productivity. In the summer, a thin layer, only a few metres thick, of the lake warms up, as you can readily find out if you dive down. This thin layer floats on top of the cold water below and does not mix with it. This upper layer is where most of the biological activity takes place. Down below, in a cold, dark, oxygen-poor netherworld, sluggish creatures make a living on the bits of dead organic material that rain down from above.

Twice a year, though, all of the water equalizes to a temperature of about 4°C. During these times, called the spring and fall turnovers, the action of the wind and waves can stir up all of the water in the lake. This accomplishes two things that are vital to life in the lake: nutrients that were languishing on the bottom get churned up and made available for the plants that live near the top, and all of the water is able to take a big gulp of oxygen. Without the physics of the turnover, the biology would be much poorer.

Animals of Algonquin

Visitors to Algonquin Park are guests in the home of 47 species of mammals (not including humans and domestic animals), 52 species of fish, 30 species of reptiles and amphibians, and thousands of species of insects. Two hundred seventy species of birds have been recorded, of which 138 are known to have bred in Algonquin. People come from around the world hoping to spot moose, deer, bears, wolves, or beaver in their native habitat, to see and hear birds, or to catch fish. "The Explorer's Guide to Algonquin Park", by Michael Runtz, provides detailed information on when, where, and how to seek out wildlife, especially mammals and birds. In "Mammals of Algonquin Provincial Park", Dan Strickland suggests driving slowly along the highways, particularly just after sunrise or just before sunset. You can cover considerable territory this way, and the mammals are not as alarmed by a car as they are by a person in the open.

Moose

Algonquin Park Museum

Moose are Algonquin's largest and most spectacular mammals. In the summer, they can be found eating aquatic plants near lakeshores, or in cool conifer forests where they browse on trees and shrubs. In the fall mating season the forest echoes with the roars and bellows of males clashing their antlers, interspersed with moans and wails of females. Moose seek shelter under evergreens in winter, venturing into more open areas to browse tender shrubs. When spring comes, you may see moose right from your car along Highway 60, as they lick salt left from winter de-icing.

Populations of moose and deer changed during the twentieth century as the forest matured. During the first half of the century, deer were abundant because widespread logging and large forest fires created a landscape favoured by deer — lots of open areas and young forest. As fire suppression became effective and forest harvests became smaller and more selective, the forest changed into habitat more favourable to moose — deep shade under tall, well-spaced evergreens. In addition, deer carry a parasite that does not harm them, but is fatal to moose, so moose have benefited from the decline in deer populations.

Black bear

Algonquin Park Museum

Black bears roam far and wide looking for food. Omnivorous creatures, they rely heavily on leaves, nuts, and berries, but also eat insect larvae, fish, even baby deer and moose, and, rarely, people. Generally, they fear people; it is important to keep it that way. Follow park instructions carefully. While memorable to see a black bear in the wild, the best encounters are brief and at a distance.

Eastern wolf

Algonquin Park Museum

Wolves, once feared and loathed, now appeal to Algonquin Park visitors. Recent genetic research has shown that Algonquin's wolves are not the timber wolves of the north, but rather a newly-recognized species called Eastern wolves. They are believed to have ranged throughout eastern North America, preying primarily on deer. Eastern wolves have been exterminated throughout most of their range, except for a remnant population called red wolves that still inhabit parts of the gulf coast of Texas and Louisiana, and a larger population living mostly north of the Great Lakes and St. Lawrence River from Minnesota and Manitoba in the west through Quebec in the east. They prey primarily on white-tailed deer, but seek other food, particularly beaver, when deer are scarce.

Their numbers declined from the 1960s to the 1990s as Algonquin's forest matured, decreasing the amount of prime deer habitat. Many of Algonquin's wolves leave the park in winter to prey on the deer that are still plentiful in the more open land outside the park. Because of concern over the number of wolves being killed in these forays, the Government of Ontario has now banned killing wolves in a buffer zone outside Algonquin.

Few visitors ever see a wolf, as they are adept at avoiding people. However, they are happy to howl back when someone howls like a wolf, so public wolf howls have become a popular way for visitors to experience Algonquin's wolves first-hand.

Beaver

Algonquin Park Museum

Beavers, fascinating rodents, symbolize industriousness for Canadians. They have evolved a unique strategy to survive and prosper. Shallow ponds protect them from predators, so they create their own ponds by damming small streams. Then they build a lodge in the pond that has two underwater entrances. To alert its family to danger, a beaver slaps its large flat tail on the water, and everyone scurries home. They prefer poplar and birch trees for food. From a human perspective, beavers can seem quite destructive and wasteful, felling many trees and just using the leaves, buds, and tender bark of the upper branches for food, and cutting off sticks for their dams and homes. They will take down remarkably large trees, cutting long slices of wood around the trunk with their front teeth. Their teeth keep growing to keep from getting worn down, so beavers must gnaw trees, or their teeth will grow too long.

When beavers create a new pond, remarkable changes affect the local ecology. Mature trees die from the higher water table. These provide feeding opportunities for fungi, insects, and birds that eat them. The pond provides habitat for frogs, fish, ducks, kingfishers, herons, otters, and muskrats, among others. When the ponds are abandoned, the dams break down, the pond drains, and a new ecosystem, a beaver meadow, takes its place, slowly being replaced by a mature forest unless another beaver family moves in. Quite literally, busy beavers create a whole new world.

Over 270 species of **birds** have been recorded in Algonquin Park at least once. These include songbirds, woodpeckers, owls, raptors, geese, ducks, and loons.

The haunting calls of **loons** epitomize the northern wilderness. Loons have several distinct calls, all of which are weird and wonderful. You can be paddling your canoe or walking a trail, when suddenly, without warning, a loud yodel-like-call breaks the silence. Granite hills echo the sound. Listen quietly, and from somewhere far away may come an answering call. Most lakes have at least one breeding pair. Watch for a loon family out for a swim in the early evening or a baby loon riding on its mom's back. Adult loons often stretch their wings in the early morning,

Common Loon

Algonquin Park Museum

flying by with a loud whoosh-whoosh-whoosh as their wings work hard to keep their large bodies in the air. Loons can stay under water a long time and dive to great depths. Their underwater agility enables them to catch fish darting to escape.

Pileated woodpeckers, large birds with big bills sporting a distinctive red crest, add to the park's colour. Although not endangered, pileated woodpeckers require large territories, so they are not common. They may help you spot them with their shrieking calls to defend their territory or loud pecking while excavating holes to make nests and find dinner. Look carefully for their cavities in large dead or dying trees. If you are lucky, you might even get close when the busy bird is pecking away and see the heavy rain of wood chips, evidence of its hard work. They require old-growth forest, not optimum for timber production. The Ontario Ministry of Natural Resources identifies them as a "featured species" to ensure that some areas of suitable habitat are left for them throughout Ontario, despite interest in timber production over much of the province.

Pileated woodpecker

Algonquin Park Museum

More than fifty species of **fish** live in Algonquin Park waters. **Trout** have benefited most from the park's creation because they are extremely susceptible to ecological disruption. They require deep, cold, clear water with good oxygen content but a relatively low level of nutrients. This means that they are easily eliminated if the water becomes polluted, which is a problem in other parts of Ontario, but not in Algonquin.

Algonquin Park has two species of trout, Brook trout and Lake trout. Brook trout can be found in fast flowing, well-oxygenated streams as well as lakes, while Lake trout are generally confined to lakes. Both species require cold water, so in summer, they stay deep, with occasional brief hunting forays into the warm upper waters. During the spring and fall turnovers (see page 37), and in the winter below the ice, they can be found at all levels. Lake trout spawn at night in October on rocky shoals. Fertilized eggs drift down to the bottom where they remain until hatching in March and April. Brook Trout require sand or gravel beds located where spring water is upwelling. This very specialized requirement has prevented Brook trout from occupying many lakes that otherwise would be suitable for them. They spawn in November, and the female covers the fertilized eggs where they remain until they hatch between February and April.

In Algonquin the most serious threat to trout is the introduction of alien species. Smallmouth Bass were first introduced in 1899, and overwhelmed the native Brook trout in many Algonquin lakes. Northern Pike, a voracious predator, has been migrating up the Opeongo River since 1982. It quickly devours and out-competes Brook trout, and makes life much more difficult for Lake trout. Other foreign species, such as rock bass and rainbow smelt, have appeared through the illegal use of live bait.

The most colourful fish in the Park, the **Pumpkinseed,** has a golden brown to olive body that sports multicoloured spots. It is common and widespread, well adapted to nearly all of Algonquin's aquatic habitats. The best way to observe and enjoy the pumpkinseed and many other fish of Algonquin Park, is to put on a mask and swim quietly on the surface, looking down into the water. Areas with vegetation often have more fish than areas with bare bottoms. A snorkel makes it possible to breath without popping your head up all the time, fins make it easier to swim quietly, and a wetsuit is nice if the water is cold. One of the best places for snorkeling is at the mouth of the Petawawa River where it enters Lake Traverse.

The **amphibian** population of Algonquin Park consists of nine species of frogs, one toad, and six species of salamander. In recent years, many scientists argue that frogs alert us to the condition of the global ecosystem. They serve as a warning, like the canary in the coalmine. When we read of the loss of wetlands, global declines in amphibian populations, and see pictures of strangely deformed frogs, we realize that the world of frogs, and indeed all of nature, is not as robust and resilient to our abuses as we may have thought. In Algonquin Park we are still privileged to be able to listen to frog choruses in the spring and appreciate another year of froggy courting and reproduction. We have chosen the Gray Treefrog to represent the frogs of Algonquin for this book. You can hear their courtship choruses in wetlands in June. Then they move onto land, where they are most readily spotted on warm evenings hunting for the insects that are attracted to lights at campsites. Unlike other frogs, gray treefrogs can become green, gray, or brown depending on their surroundings.

The **reptile** inhabitants of Algonquin Park include nine snake and five turtle species. All Algonquin Park snakes are harmless. Don't bother them. The Garter snake, the most common, is the one you are most likely to see. The Snapping and Painted turtles are the most commonly observed turtles. Snapping turtles are large and exhibit primal reptilian aggression. They like to lay their eggs in roadside sand, so both adults and hatchlings sometimes become road kill.

Painted turtle

The Painted turtle is more placid and photogenic. They can be seen basking at the edge of a lake or pond on sunny days. Basking is important to both turtles and snakes, because they are cold-blooded animals. They do not maintain an elevated body temperature as birds and mammals do. This makes it possible for them to survive on much less food. But they must be warm to be active, so they bask to absorb a dose of free solar energy to warm up for important activities like mating and feeding.

Insects interact with human visitors to the Park more than any other kind of animal. Like flowers, many insects have brief seasons during the spring, summer, or fall when they become adults, are present in large numbers for mating, and then disappear as eggs, larvae, or pupae for another year. Of the thousands of insect species that live in Algonquin Park, we feature three of the prettiest and most common.

Canadian Tiger Swallowtail butterfly

Algonquin Park Museum

The Canadian Tiger Swallowtail butterfly has adapted to feeding on the birch and poplar trees that are common in Algonquin Park. Watch for these distinctive yellow and black butterflies in open areas and that have flowers to provide nectar. Their daily routine starts with a warming sunbath to provide the get up and go to forage for nectar. The nectar in turn provides energy for an afternoon of flying around in search of mates. You may also find clusters of swallowtails at the roadside. These are males, consuming roadside salt, to replace the sodium compounds that are transferred to the females as part of the mating process.

River Jewelwing

Algonquin Park Museum

Dragonflies flit around Algonquin's many lakes all summer long. These agile little helicopters rival the Red Baron's flight manoeuvres while pursuing their favourite meal, the dreaded mosquito. Watch closely at dusk to see the dragonflies swoop and swallow. Before they emerge as adults, dragonfly nymphs are aggressive meat-eaters that live in the water. They eat tadpoles, as well as other prey. As adults, however, the tables are turned. Frogs become the predators and dragonflies the prey! The adult male whitefaced meadowfly is particularly notable since it is bright red when viewed from above. This is a common dragonfly near lakes and ponds of Algonquin from July to September.

White-faced meadowfly

Allen Chartier

Damselflies, unlike dragonflies, fold their wings behind them when they alight. Brilliant metallic green River Jewelwings dart and perch near rivers and streams during the first half of the summer.

Human history

As the glaciers retreated northward and a spruce-pine forest crept in, caribou followed the trees. The earliest people followed the caribou. Archeologists have found projectile points left near ancient campfires from as early as 8600 BC. Another seven thousand years passed before the people made and used pottery. Corn, the earliest agriculture crop, arrived around 500 AD in southern Ontario, but beans, sunflowers, squash, and tobacco were not cultivated until about 1200.

At the time Jacques Cartier sailed up the St. Lawrence in 1535, the area was inhabited by Algonquian-speaking hunter-gatherers to the north of the St. Lawrence River and Iroquois agriculturalists along the river and to the south. An attempt to establish a permanent settlement failed in 1543 and there was no European exploration on the St. Lawrence past Québec until Champlain arrived in 1603. By then the Iroquois had disappeared; the native persons he met spoke Algonquian languages

In 1613, a trip up the Ottawa Valley brought Champlain face-to-face with the Algonquian-speaking Kichesippirini, the People of the Great River. The Kichesippirini inhabited the rugged uplands that comprise Algonquin Park. Long-standing enmity between the Algonquin and Iroquois brought sporadic warfare. Impressed with the deadly firepower of the French, the Kichesippirini requested military help from Champlain. Seeking them as allies, he obliged. Before long the native people were caught up in European geo-politics: the Algonquins allied with the French and the Iroquois with the British.

The Iroquois, with their five-nation confederacy, killed and dispersed most of their Algonquian-speaking enemies between 1647 and 1653. Surviving Algonquins fled to French missions or into forests north of the Ottawa River to escape. Disease decimated those who chose refuge in the missions, while starvation undoubtedly stalked those who did not.

For the next hundred years, the French and British continued to vie for land and the fur trade. The fortunes of the Algonquin ebbed and flowed with the fortunes of the French. The British ultimately prevailed. They issued a number of proclamations intended to protect the land and rights of the Algonquin. These good intentions only lasted, however, until land was needed for refugees from the American Revolution and the timber resources became too tempting to leave alone. Inexorably, Europeans displaced native inhabitants. In many cases, the Crown claimed title to land through treaties signed with individual tribes, but there was no treaty with the Algonquin. For decades the Algonquin petitioned various authorities over the loss of their land. Usually these petitions received sympathy, but no action. Finally, the Crown established two reserves for the Algonquins: one near Maniwaki,

Algonquin Park Museum

The Algonquin people, the original inhabitants of the Ottawa Valley and the Algonquin uplands, took advantage of the extensive waterways for travel. Their boat design, the canoe, is now used throughout the world.

Québec, in 1851, a small property beside Golden Lake in Ontario in 1873, and several reserves north of Maniwaki in the twentieth century. No one considered native interests when establishing Algonquin Park in 1893, and traditional activities within its boundaries were initially outlawed. At present, the Algonquin people are negotiating a land claim agreement with the governments of Ontario and Canada. Hunting, trapping, and fishing within Algonquin Park are carried out under interim agreements pending a final resolution.

The nineteenth century approach to development was to lease large tracts of forest to timber barons who would cut trees and open the land to make way for settlement and farming. British appetite for Canadian timber seemed insatiable. Tall, straight, white pine made fine masts with which Britannia could rule the waves.

Loggers munched into the forests north of Toronto and up the Ottawa Valley like hordes of hungry insects. Alexander McDonnell began surveying the timber along the Madawaska, Bonnechere, and Petawawa rivers in the 1820s. Before long, thousands of logs floated downstream in the spring flood every year. After depleting the pines, the government gave the land to indigent, but eager immigrants for farming. Elaborate schemes

Algonquin Park Museum Archives #2193 (Eva Middleton)

Middleton farm, an early pioneer settlement. Note the many rock outcrops and deforested landscape. Algonquin Park was instituted to prevent the entire area from becoming like this.

lured many from lives of poverty in Europe to a new misery in North America. The Canadian Shield proved particularly unsuited for farming, but enthusiasm for settling the Algonquin Park area remained undampened in Toronto and Ottawa, despite decades of watching broken immigrants abandon failed farms along settlement roads that drilled into the interior.

By the 1880s, little was left of the original forests in eastern North America. Erosion, spring floods, and summer droughts bedeviled the region as loggers cleared watershed after watershed and immigrants scratched out marginal farms. Eventually, economists, foresters, and early environmentalists became alarmed and the tide started to turn. Noting that the headwaters of several important rivers originate in the Algonquin highlands, visionaries Robert Phipps and Alexander Kirkwood warned of the danger of allowing settlement and farming to sweep across this area. The park was established in 1893 with three goals: to provide a continuous supply of timber; to protect important Ontario rivers; and to provide a refuge for wildlife, particularly deer, moose, beaver, marten, and fisher.

Few would have thought of a nature preserve when viewing the industrial parts of the Algonquin Park landscape at the time of its creation. Log stockpiles were surrounded by large areas containing little but stumps and shrubs. Industrial logging pocked the landscape with sawmills, sawdust burners, and rail yards. Even larger tracts were burned over — the result of carelessness and ineffective fire fighting.

Since Algonquin Park was founded in 1893 logging has become more selective and sustainable and is not allowed in sizable wilderness areas and nature reserves. Large resorts have been replaced by more modest accommodations. Today, Algonquin forests are younger than they were before the loggers arrived, but the three main goals have been achieved. Wildlife and their habitats abound; plentiful water runs pure; and the forests still feed millions of dollars into the economy.

Algonquin Park helped establish Canada's reputation as a land rich in forests and sparkling lakes, abundant with big game, big fish, and fascinating wildlife. People come from afar to experience raw nature first hand; few leave disappointed. Artists, led particularly by Tom Thompson and the Group of

Algonquin Park Museum

Logging practices have evolved throughout the history of Algonquin Park. Selective logging thins the trees, but retains a significant tree cover, as shown in the vertical view above. Skilled tree markers select the trees to be harvested (inset).

Seven ignited interest in the Canadian wilderness when they visited Algonquin and evoked its spirit in their paintings. They touched urban souls, who came flocking in droves to see for themselves. Early tourist amenities were rustic but comfortable. Hotels were easily accessible by train. Boating and fishing were popular from the outset. Some hearty souls, usually men who already had experience in the bush, traveled to the back woods by canoe. Before long, entire families were discovering the joys of "roughing it" on canoe trips to the interior.

Algonquin Park quickly became a laboratory where scientists worked to understand individual species and complex interactions among animals and plants. The work of these pioneers and their colleagues around the world gave birth to the science of ecology. Interpretive programs share these scientific findings with park visitors. These researchers and teachers deserve credit for putting the concepts of "ecology" and "ecosystem" into everyday vocabulary.

This is a land of many uses and many demands: clean water, forest products, wildlife, scientific research, recreation, and even spiritual renewal. Ontario Parks, part of the Ministry of Natural Resources, juggles these diverse needs. The planning process brings in information from biologists, foresters, geologists, archeologists, historians, resource scientists, managers, and the general public. With such diverse interests it is not surprising that the planning process is contentious. No one is entirely satisfied. But the results are good. Let's go enjoy it.

Algonquin Park Museum

Morning mists rise from the warm surface waters of Algonquin Park lakes after clear cool nights.

Algonquin beckons

Enough armchair traveling! Whether you visit Algonquin Park for a day, a week, or a month, you will never run out of things to see and do. The best place to begin is at the Visitor Centre, located at kilometre 43 along Highway 60, measured from the West Gate. Here you will find dioramas and other displays that illustrate the history and ecology of the park. An observation deck offers a panoramic view of a black spruce wetland, with telescopes for close-up views. You may want to check out the bookstore and then head out to the trails and lakes.

Algonquin Park Museum

Visitors explore nature along the spruce bog trail.

Nature trails

Seventeen nature trails, 14 of which start from parking lots along Highway 60, lead you quickly to exceptional vistas, as well as forests and bogs, lakes and streams. Dan Strickland, former Chief Naturalist for Algonquin Park, has written a delightful and informative guide for each trail, all beautifully illustrated with ink drawings by Howard Coneybeare. Each trail highlights a particular theme of the human and natural history of the park. Some trails are short and easy, and some are long and arduous; use the table below to plan your hikes.

The three northern trails, Barron Canyon, Brent Crater, and Berm Lake, are accessible from roads that join Highway 17.

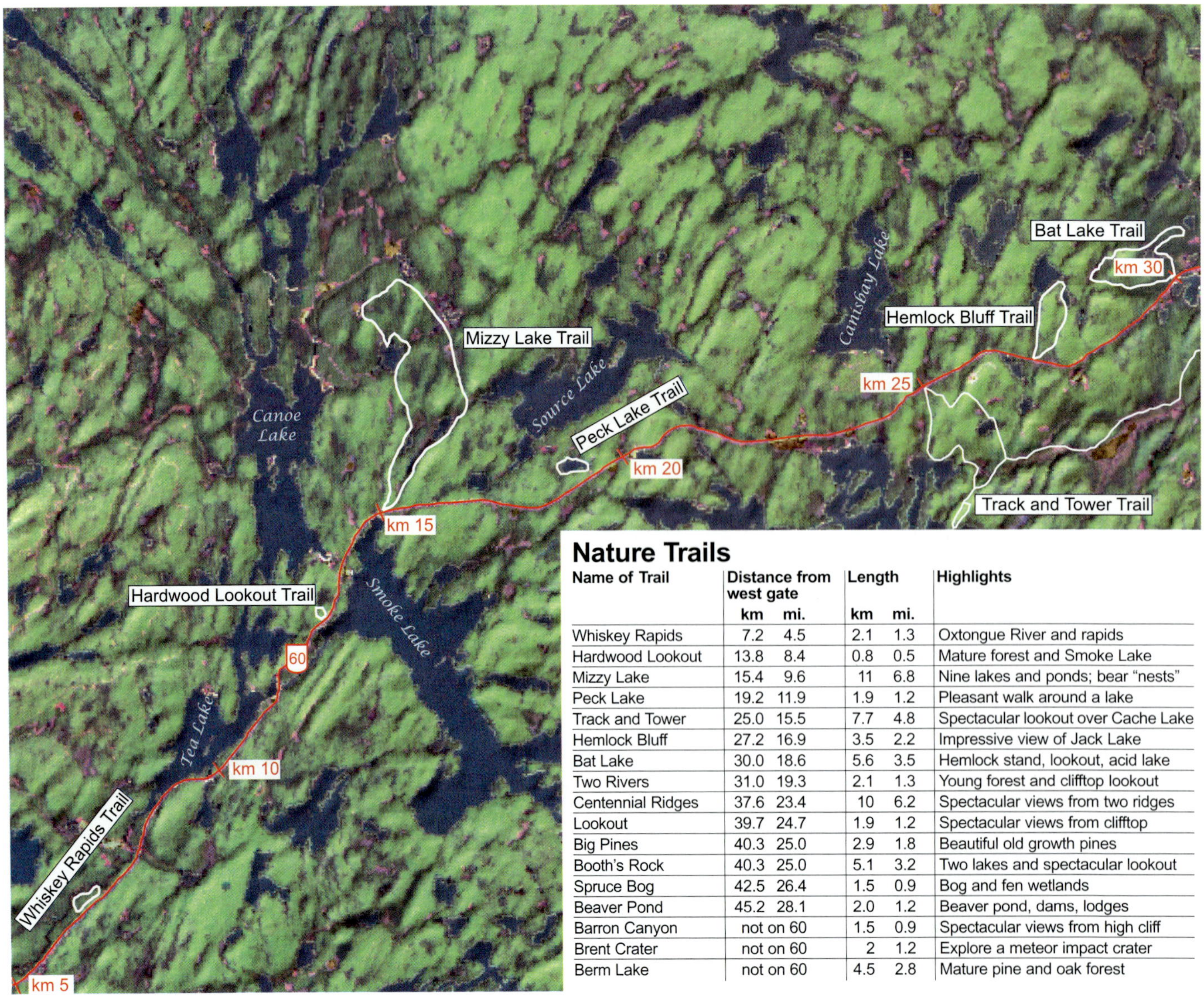

Nature Trails

Name of Trail	Distance from west gate		Length		Highlights
	km	mi.	km	mi.	
Whiskey Rapids	7.2	4.5	2.1	1.3	Oxtongue River and rapids
Hardwood Lookout	13.8	8.4	0.8	0.5	Mature forest and Smoke Lake
Mizzy Lake	15.4	9.6	11	6.8	Nine lakes and ponds; bear "nests"
Peck Lake	19.2	11.9	1.9	1.2	Pleasant walk around a lake
Track and Tower	25.0	15.5	7.7	4.8	Spectacular lookout over Cache Lake
Hemlock Bluff	27.2	16.9	3.5	2.2	Impressive view of Jack Lake
Bat Lake	30.0	18.6	5.6	3.5	Hemlock stand, lookout, acid lake
Two Rivers	31.0	19.3	2.1	1.3	Young forest and clifftop lookout
Centennial Ridges	37.6	23.4	10	6.2	Spectacular views from two ridges
Lookout	39.7	24.7	1.9	1.2	Spectacular views from clifftop
Big Pines	40.3	25.0	2.9	1.8	Beautiful old growth pines
Booth's Rock	40.3	25.0	5.1	3.2	Two lakes and spectacular lookout
Spruce Bog	42.5	26.4	1.5	0.9	Bog and fen wetlands
Beaver Pond	45.2	28.1	2.0	1.2	Beaver pond, dams, lodges
Barron Canyon	not on 60		1.5	0.9	Spectacular views from high cliff
Brent Crater	not on 60		2	1.2	Explore a meteor impact crater
Berm Lake	not on 60		4.5	2.8	Mature pine and oak forest

Taking a break during a canoe trip to the interior.

Canoeing

Canoeing is the most popular way to visit the park interior; indeed, Algonquin Park is often considered synonymous with canoe trips. Solitude, simplicity, friendship, fishing, birding, renewing contact with nature, or achieving a physical challenge are among the joys people mention of canoeing. Reservations are required, but even during the busiest time of summer there is no sense of crowding. *Canoe Routes of Algonquin Park* can be purchased at the Visitor Centre bookstore or from outfitters. This excellent map and guide identifies many natural and cultural points of interest that can only be accessed by canoeing the interior.

Backpacking and skiing

Algonquin Park also offers excellent opportunities for backpacking and skiing. The backpacking trails offer circuit hikes with varying loop lengths. The Western Uplands and Highland trails take you through typical upland topography, while the Eastern Pines trail highlights the lower east side. Algonquin is a winter wonderland, and a skiing visit is highly recommended. January and early February can be bitter cold, but fine conditions are common from late February to late March, particularly on bright clear days. It will seem peaceful and quiet, but an abundance of tracks reveal that many animals are going about their business.

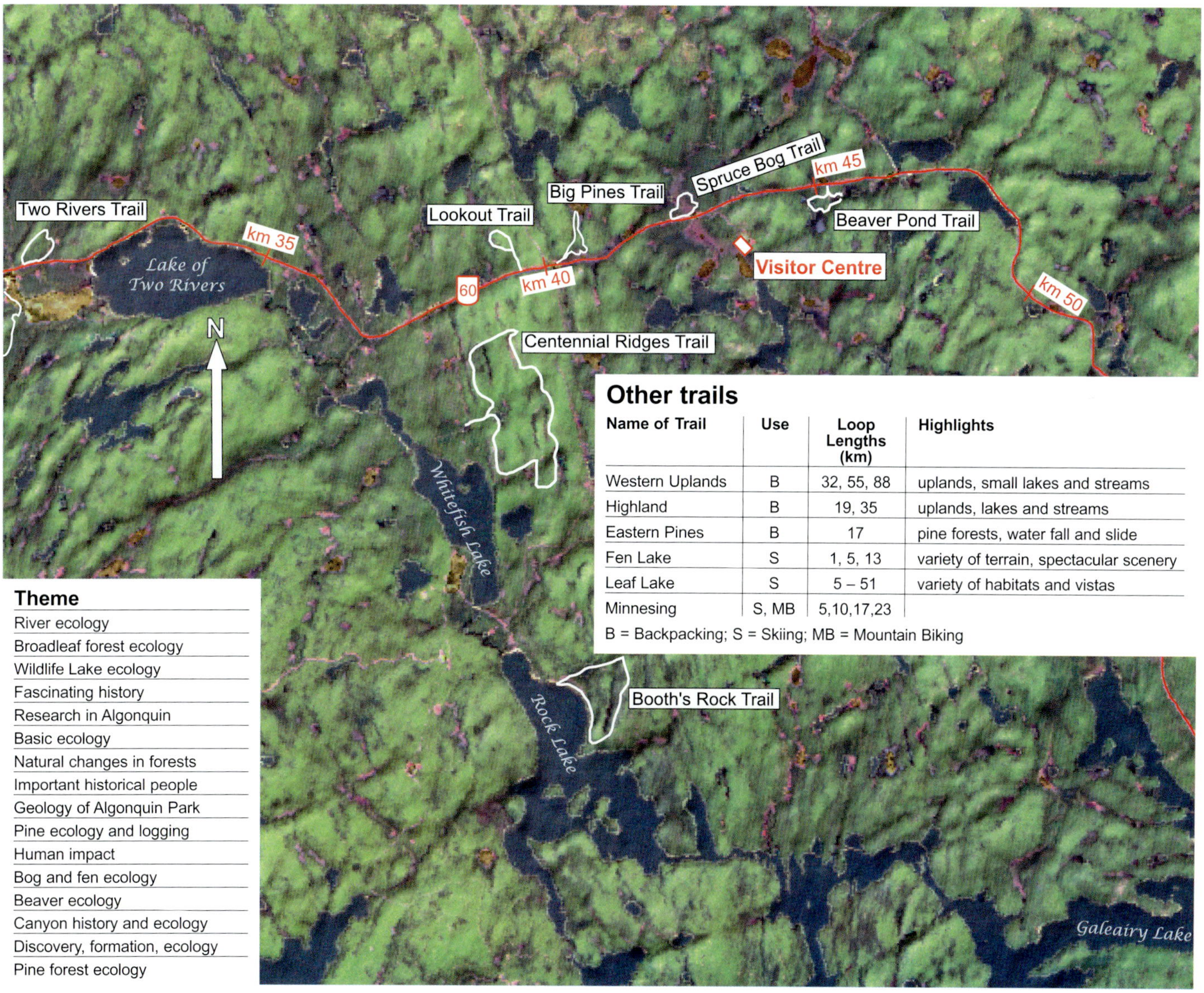

Other trails

Name of Trail	Use	Loop Lengths (km)	Highlights
Western Uplands	B	32, 55, 88	uplands, small lakes and streams
Highland	B	19, 35	uplands, lakes and streams
Eastern Pines	B	17	pine forests, water fall and slide
Fen Lake	S	1, 5, 13	variety of terrain, spectacular scenery
Leaf Lake	S	5 – 51	variety of habitats and vistas
Minnesing	S, MB	5,10,17,23	

B = Backpacking; S = Skiing; MB = Mountain Biking

Theme

River ecology
Broadleaf forest ecology
Wildlife Lake ecology
Fascinating history
Research in Algonquin
Basic ecology
Natural changes in forests
Important historical people
Geology of Algonquin Park
Pine ecology and logging
Human impact
Bog and fen ecology
Beaver ecology
Canyon history and ecology
Discovery, formation, ecology
Pine forest ecology

Looking to the future

In the last 10,000 years, Earth has witnessed the return of life toward the poles as the ice age ended. In the last 3000 years or so, human populations have spread across the globe and increased dramatically. As populations have increased, nature has been suppressed, repressed, and, in large cities, virtually extinguished.

Parks like Algonquin have been established, in part, as an attempt to preserve nature. What do we mean by "nature"? Biologists today respond by emphasizing ecosystem integrity and biological diversity.

Ecosystem integrity means that an ecosystem is functioning much as it would in the absence of major alteration by human actions. Biological diversity means that all of the animal and plant species originally present in an area are still there, and are not in danger of dying out through human actions. By these measures, Algonquin Park receives high marks, while also providing recreational and economic opportunities. Can this continue? Can you help?

An island of nature in a sea of development?

The establishment of many natural parks in the last 125 years has bought time, but it is not a permanent solution. Experience has shown that nature cannot survive as an island in a sea of development. Algonquin's wolves migrate out of the park in pursuit of deer; what happens to them outside the boundaries affects their populations inside the park. Algonquin's lakes are very sensitive to acid rain; only increasingly stringent measures to control sulphur emissions will enable the aquatic ecosystems to survive. Algonquin also faces a long-term threat from the increasing development of "cottage country". Dense roads and high traffic outside the park could decimate wildlife and slowly smother the little island of wilderness in a shroud of smog. Road and cottage development is currently most severe toward the south, but could easily encircle and strangle Algonquin Park in the next 100 years.

Climate changes affect everything

Global climate change is a reality. Algonquin is warming; the ecology is changing. Northern species at the southern limit of their range in Algonquin may leave, and more southerly species may infiltrate the park. The real unknown is precipitation. With enough moisture, Algonquin will remain green and lush. If not, today's forests will die through drought and fire. In time grasses and shrubs will encroach. Current efforts to ameliorate human-caused climate change, notably the Kyoto Protocol, are not aggressive enough to prevent some more warming over the next 100 years. Predictions beyond that time frame are only guesswork, because scientists cannot predict our response in upcoming decades to the clear warnings before us now.

Threats specific to Algonquin Park

Within Algonquin Park, roads create problems. Unauthorized use of interior roads with all-terrain vehicles and snowmobiles facilitates illegal hunting and fishing. Park authorities continue to devise new ways to deal with these problems.

Invasive species are serious threats to ecosystem integrity and biodiversity. The beloved ladybug has already been supplanted by an Asian invader that has pushed out the native species. We will have to work hard to avoid serious damage by other aliens such as the Asian longhorn beetle and the zebra mussel.

What can you do?

It is easy to feel powerless in the face of so many threats. But these threats are a consequence of our collective actions, and they can be reduced through our collective actions. Here are some basics:

- Be an advocate for a healthy environment: Do more than your fair share, and encourage your friends and neighbours to do their part too.
- Insist on good air and water quality where you live. This will let politicians know these are important to you and Algonquin Park will benefit as well.
- Reduce excess consumption of energy and goods, and encourage friends and neighbours to do the same.
- Watch your waste: recycle everything you can and avoid using products that are harmful to the environment.
- The cost of fuel and electricity are going to increase. Appreciate the positive aspects of this trend, rather than pressuring politicians to resist it through artificial subsidies and other unsustainable measures. Emphasize more efficient use of the energy we have, rather than new sources of supply.
- Support restrictions on motor vehicle use and access inside Algonquin Park and restrictions on road building outside the park.
- Support planning and restrictions on the use of land outside of Algonquin Park to prevent dense development and habitat fragmentation.
- Support the Algonquin to Adirondacks initiative to make human development more compatible with the needs of nature in the corridor that links Algonquin Park to Adirondack Park in New York state.
- Become involved: devote some of your time and energy to a bright future for Algonquin Park. Relevant organizations and addresses are given on the next page.

Organizations that are involved in managing, supporting, and planning for Algonquin Park

The Friends of Algonquin Park
Box 248
Whitney, Ontario
K0J 2M0
(613) 637-2828
http://www.algonquinpark.on.ca/

Local Citizens' Committee
Algonquin Park Forest
Box 730
Minden, Ontario
K0M 2K0
(705) 286-3555

Algonquin Eco Watch
RR # 1
Spring Bay
Ontario
P0P 2B0
http://www.algonquin-eco-watch.com/

The Ontario Parks website http://www.ontarioparks.com provides opportunities for email input. Click "feedback" on the home page.

Write the
Ontario Minister of Natural Resources
6th Floor, Room 6630
Whitney Block
99 Wellesley St. W.
Toronto, Ontario
M7A 1W3

Ontario residents can also write their local member of provincial parliament (MPP) to express their concerns and wishes.

Additional reading and sources used in preparation of this book

Geology

Carr, S. D., R. M. Easton, R. A. Jamieson, and N. G. Culshaw, 2000. "Geologic transect across the Grenville orogen of Ontario and New York", Canadian Journal of Earth Science, 37, pp 193-216.

Chapman, L. J., 1975. "The physiography of the Georgian Bay-Ottawa Valley area of Southern Ontario", Ontario Division of Mines Geoscience Report 128.

Davidson, A., 1998. "An overview of the Grenville Province geology, Canadian Shield", in *Geology of the Precambrian Superior and Grenville Provinces and Precambrian Fossils in North America*, S. B. Lucas and M. R. St. Onge, coordinators, Geological Survey of Canada, Geology of Canada, no. 7, pp 205-270.

Eyles, Nick, 2002. *Ontario Rocks: three billion years of environmental change*, Fitzhenry and Whiteside, Markham, Ontario, Canada, 339 pp.

Ficher, Lynn S. 2003. "The Wilson Cycle", course notes http://csmres.jmu.edu/geollab/Fichter/Wilson/Wilson.html, James Madison University.

Ford, M. J., 1986. Specific areas of earth science significance within Algonquin Provincial Park, Ontario Geological Society Open File Report.

Guillet, G. R., 1969. "Algonquin Provincial Park, a geological guide to Highway 60", Ontario Department of Mines, MP29, 44 pp.

Kious, W. J., and R. I. Tilling, 1996. *This Dynamic Earth: the Story of Plate Tectonics*, United States Geological Society, 77 pp.

Rockwell, David, 1998. *The Nature of North America*, The Berkley Publishing Company, 379 pp.

Thurston, P. C. *et al.* (ed), 1991. *Geology of Ontario*, Ontario Ministry of Northern Development and Mines.

Ecology

Begon, Michael, J. L. Harper, and C. R. Townsend, 1996. *Ecology: Individuals, Populations, and Communities*, 3rd edition, Blackwell Science, Oxford, UK.

Campbell, Neil A., 1996. *Biology*, 4th edition, The Benjamin/Cummings Publishing Company, New York.

Chambers, B. A., B. J. Naylor, J. Nieppola, B. Merchant, and P. Uhlig, 1997. *Field Guide to Forest Ecosystems of Central Ontario*, Ontario Ministry of Natural Resources.

Quinn, Norm, 2002. *Algonquin Wildlife: Lessons in Survival*, Natural Heritage/Natural History Inc., Toronto, Canada, 246 pp.

Raven, Peter H., and G. B. Johnson, 1995. *Understanding Biology*, Wm. C. Brown Publishers, Toronto, Canada.

Raven, Peter H., Ray F. Evert, and Susan E. Eichhorn, 1992. *Biology of Plants*, 5th edition, Worth Publishers, New York.

Runtz, Michael, 1993. *The Explorer's Guide to Algonquin Park*, revised edition, Stoddart Publishing, Toronto, Canada, 184 pp.

Strickland, Dan, Trail Guides for the 14 trails tabulated on page 44, available from the bookstore of the Algonquin Visitor Centre.

The Friends of Algonquin publishes the following titles that are available from the bookstore at the Visitor Centre:

Birds of Algonquin Provincial Park, by Dan Strickland, 2002.

Butterflies of Algonquin Provincial Park, by Gard W. Otis, 1994.

Fishes of Algonquin Provincial Park, by Nicholas E. Mandrak and E. J. Crossman, 2003.

Fishing in Algonquin Provincial Park, by Dan Strickland, 2002.

Insects of Algonquin Provincial Park, by Steve Marshall, 1997.

Mammals of Algonquin Provincial Park, by Dan Strickland and Russell J. Rutter, drawings by Howard Coneybeare, 2002.

Reptiles and Amphibians of Algonquin Provincial Park, by Ronald J. Brooks, Dan Strickland, and Russell J. Rutter, 2003.

Trees of Algonquin Provincial Park, by Dan Strickland, 1987.

Wildflowers of Algonquin Provincial Park, by Dan Strickland and John LeVay, 1986.

Human History

Harris, R. Cole, and G. J. Matthews, 1987. *Historical Atlas of Canada*, Volume I, "From the Beginning to 1800", University of Toronto Press, Toronto, Canada, 198 pp.

Hessel, Peter, 1993. *The Algonkin Nation*, Kichesipi Books, Arnprior, Ontario, Canada, 106 pp.

Holmes, Joan and Assoc. Inc, 1993. "Algonquins of Golden Lake Claim", Contract Report for Ontario Ministry of Native Affairs.

Saunders, Audrey, 1963. *Algonquin Story*, Ontario Department of Lands and Forests, 196 pp plus five maps.

Strickland, Dan, 2000. "Centennial Ridges Trail Guide", The Friends of Algonquin Park, 16 pp.

Wright, H. Eleanor, 2003. *Trailblazers of Algonquin Park*, HEW Enterprises, Eganville, Ontario, Canada, 242 pp.

Index